Cambridge Elements ≡

Elements in Global Urban History
edited by
Michael Goebel
Graduate Institute Geneva
Tracy Neumann
Wayne State University
Joseph Ben Prestel
Freie Universität Berlin

FOODWAYS IN THE TWENTIETH-CENTURY CITY

Maria-Aparecida Lopes
California State University, Fresno
María Cecilia Zuleta
El Colegio de México

Shaftesbury Road, Cambridge CB2 8EA, United Kingdom

One Liberty Plaza, 20th Floor, New York, NY 10006, USA

477 Williamstown Road, Port Melbourne, VIC 3207, Australia

314–321, 3rd Floor, Plot 3, Splendor Forum, Jasola District Centre, New Delhi – 110025, India

103 Penang Road, #05–06/07, Visioncrest Commercial, Singapore 238467

Cambridge University Press is part of Cambridge University Press & Assessment, a department of the University of Cambridge.

We share the University's mission to contribute to society through the pursuit of education, learning and research at the highest international levels of excellence.

www.cambridge.org
Information on this title: www.cambridge.org/9781009500876

DOI: 10.1017/9781009057516

When citing this work, please include a reference to the DOI 10.1017/9781009057516

First published 2024

A catalogue record for this publication is available from the British Library

ISBN 978-1-009-50087-6 Hardback
ISBN 978-1-009-06031-8 Paperback
ISSN 2632-3206 (online)
ISSN 2632-3192 (print)

Cambridge University Press & Assessment has no responsibility for the persistence or accuracy of URLs for external or third-party internet websites referred to in this publication and does not guarantee that any content on such websites is, or will remain, accurate or appropriate.

Foodways in the Twentieth-Century City

Elements in Global Urban History

DOI: 10.1017/9781009057516
First published online: December 2024

Maria-Aparecida Lopes
California State University, Fresno

María Cecilia Zuleta
El Colegio de México

Author for correspondence: Maria-Aparecida Lopes, mlopes@csufresno.edu

Abstract: *Foodways in the Twentieth-Century City* explores a fundamental question through the lens of the modern metropolis: How did the experience of food and eating evolve throughout the twentieth century? In answering this query, this Element examines significant changes in the production, distribution, and consumption of food in cities worldwide. It takes a comprehensive view of foodways, encompassing the material, institutional, and sociocultural conditions that shaped food's journey from farm to table. The work delves into everyday practices like buying, selling, cooking, and eating, both at home and in public spaces. Central themes include local and global food governance and food access inequality as urban communities, markets, and governments navigated the complex landscape of abundance and scarcity. This Element highlights the unique dynamics of urban food supply and consumption over time.

Keywords: food consumption, food governance, urban food markets, food struggles, supermarket, technology and new foods

ISBNs: 9781009500876 (HB), 9781009060318 (PB), 9781009057516 (OC)
ISSNs: 2632-3206 (online), 2632-3192 (print)

Contents

Introduction

This Element explores a fundamental question through the modern city lens: How did the contours of the food/eating experience evolve over the twentieth century? In answering this query, *Foodways in the Twentieth-Century City* considers changes in food production, processing, and retailing that brought foodstuffs to the urban table. As importantly, it investigates contexts in which food did not arrive in urban centers and local and transnational efforts to mitigate scarcity. Food supply was a core function of city governments. This work studies how municipal structures of provision (public markets, slaughter-houses) and ideologies facilitated – or did not – dwellers' access to the primary means of subsistence. Diverse public and private interests (labor, industrial, commercial) at the local, national, and global levels converged in cities, producing a set of expectations and eating behaviors of the urban residents. Looking at cities as case studies, we highlight how locals interacted with novel policies and technologies, acquiring goods to sustain their lives. One central theme that weaves throughout the work is food access inequality. Food partaking was and remains an uneven urban experience. If, in the early 1900s, lack of refrigeration limited dwellers' ability to enjoy perishables, in the 1950s, supermarket innovation catered to select motorized customers. In this respect, we employ a comprehensive understanding of *foodways* encompassing material, social, and ideological conditions that enable food to travel from farm to table, including urbanites' everyday practices as they buy, sell, cook, and eat food at home and on their cities' streets.

Drawing from myriad qualitative studies, *Foodways in the Twentieth-Century City* investigates practices, systems, ideas, institutions, and technologies that supported food circulation to cities. Our focus on these processes stems from a basic understanding: twentieth-century city dwellers could not live off the land; their food had to be grown and (for the most part) processed elsewhere, either in the hinterland or in distant territories, reaching cities through intricate local, regional, and global networks. As the twentieth-century metropolis grew in size and population, less food came from its immediate environs. But cities experienced these processes differently according to geography and extant political economies. Inland conurbations like Paris and Mexico City have consistently relied more on their hinterlands than have cities such as London and Rio de Janeiro. What is more, despite constant regulations that sought to draw a clear line separating city and country, urban agriculture remained integral to the city provision. Indeed, public administrators and private companies incentivized and promoted urban farming and green belts to provide goods and land ownership experience to the poor, countering rampant urbanization. The current local food movement (which is also global) is yet another challenge to rural-urban dichotomies.

It is undeniable that the urban-eating experience in the late twentieth century was one of homogeneous tastes and eating behaviors. We seek to unveil how this came to be, starting with the globalization of the late 1800s, when empires and ideologies worked in tandem to promote and expand certain foodstuffs and eating practices worldwide – think of the hygiene movement of the early 1900s and the endorsement of milk consumption that accompanied it. The work then examines the food order that emerged after World War II, which once again brought concepts and policies on ideal foodstuffs to the fore. It ends with the most recent phases of globalization, which strengthened supermarkets as the leading urban food retailer – but certainly not the only one – and popularized frozen and convenient foods to the average consumer. This Element is chronologically organized; while some themes overlap, others span different periods. During the long twentieth century, structural transformations accelerated the pace with which goods traveled across oceans, but as we will see, ideals and technologies operate in different places at different rhythms. Supermarket chains, for instance, developed first in Latin America, with US expansion in the region, and later in other parts of the globe. In considering diverse paths, we challenge diffusion center notions – whether the United States or another empire – and narratives of progress (material or otherwise).

The study interlaces several recurrent concerns over how, when, and where urban industrial workers managed to eat outside their houses – as one expects, men and women fared such constraints differently; how technology shaped the modern kitchen and food retailing; how transnational ideas about good eating permeated policies in every corner of the globe; how municipal institutions of food supply evolved; and how urban consumers' eating habits shifted. This Element examines those topics in relational terms across diverse places and conjunctures; its analytical framework privileges cities as sites in which various levels of provision governance landed, underscoring the enormous amount of work, administration, and marketing networks required to produce, distribute, and make food available in everyday urban life worldwide. It also highlights the intrinsic relationship between food and society, reflecting how trade and peoples' movements gave birth to hybrid foodways. Consider massive migrations in the age of imperialism and, in the most recent globalization, the explosive urbanization that accompanied it. On both occasions, those exchanges were implicitly or explicitly negotiated, contested, and readapted to local realities.

The cities the reader will encounter in *Foodways in the Twentieth-Century City* were not hierarchically selected. We were less concerned with their place in the national/global economy than with showcasing a wide array of connected or strikingly different experiences. Latin American cities figure preeminently in this study partly because of our backgrounds and expertise. Capital cities are also central to our argument; their significance lies in their commercial and demographic primacy and ability to centralize administration and government functions. Food has always been central to the social contract and urban governance. As numerous examples in this work demonstrate, adequate food supplies and healthy eating were (and are) matters of political legitimacy and, as such, concern municipal authorities, national governments, and international organizations.

In the past century, regular boom-and-bust cycles generated food abundance and shortages, over which urban authorities (even national governments) had limited control, given global pressure on domestic supplies and prices. Such an exposure to international market forces also reveals a phenomenon utterly familiar to the twentieth-first-century reader: skepticism over the provenance of common foods and food chains. In the twentieth century, in one way or another, consumers themselves were always involved in food matters, not only for their sustenance but also as a sphere of agency and contention. Underlying so-called food riots in cities were political and citizenship-related demands. The availability (or not) of food and the act of food buying and eating (when, where, and how) contributed to regime resistance in East Berlin and Moscow and the segregated urban South of the United States. This is also a story about how urbanities leveraged food and food spaces to muster their agency in food governance in cities across the globe.

This Element is organized into five sections. Sections 1 and 2 examine how the increased production and circulation of commodities, and mass migrations during the late 1800s homogenized certain foodstuffs and feeding policies for urban residents worldwide. Section 3 explores local governments and citizens' strategies to cope with economic and wartime crises that challenged extant food provision schemes. In the post–World War II era, industrialization and planned economics led to a new global food order and nutritional transition, once again inciting concern over how to feed an ever-growing urban population. Section 4 considers these developments across cities in the socialist and capitalist blocs and beyond these confines. In the last century, the truly revolutionary change in urban food provision was the supermarket, for its capacity to alter the supply chain from farm to table and adaptability to local conditions. Section 5 examines the rise and implementation of supermarkets, and the permanence of traditional retailing forms.

In 1900, 16 percent of the world's population lived in cities; one hundred years later, three times as much did so, albeit with striking geographic variations. At the dawn of the twentieth century, the United States and

Europe concentrated most urban centers; in the early 2000s, they were in Asia, Africa, and Latin America, and the trend continues. Over the century, metropolises worldwide made enormous strides in expanding infrastructure services (potable water and cooking fuel, and food inspections) and refurbishing public markets and wholesalers, while technologies brought new retail formats to the urban grid and kitchen equipment to homes. Urban dwellers of the early 1900s would not recognize many of these gadgets, and much less convenient goods, displayed in commercial supermarkets and corner stores on both sides of the equator today; they would, unfortunately, be familiar with pervasive food access inequalities in cities that remain as segregated as they were a century ago.

1 The Enduring Challenge: Feeding the Urban Multitude

In the late nineteenth-century city, every step involved in bringing food from farm to table underwent a complete change. From the 1880s to the 1920s, electric and fossil-based technology accelerated industrialization, transformed markets, and refashioned urban centers on a global scale. Likewise, new transport and navigation technologies increased the movement of people and foodstuffs worldwide. Old, colonial, and new cities, such as Havana, Shanghai, Los Angeles, Chicago, São Paulo, and Buenos Aires, attracted migrants from transoceanic lands, rural hinterlands, and nearby provinces. As they settled, newcomers challenged extant working conditions and repurposed urban landscapes; amid inadequate essential services, cities became ripe for social tension. Urban living changed fast – and so did foodways. Across the globe, local authorities enhanced or developed public works, waste management, and food distribution schemes particularly for the poor and migrants. They set wholesale and retail trade rules and established codes to improve sanitation and food safety. In doing so, these administrators expected to shape urban dwellers' diets, from what, where, and when they ate to how they cooked their food. This section examines the challenges municipalities faced adapting cities to fin de siècle modernity and supplying food to an ever-growing population.

Modernizing Urban Food Supply

Public and private agents developed a complex set of local, supra-regional, and transnational networks, institutions, and infrastructures to provide food to cities. Fulfilling centuries-old mandates to oversee dwellers' well-being, urban governments controlled myriad services, including sanitation and food provision. They managed food markets, granaries, slaughterhouses, milk depots, and urban gardens; supervised trading networks and vendors; and oversaw food and drinking water quality. Public granaries had been at the center of urban provision for millennia. Granaries performed multiple functions of common interest: storying grains (to protect them from fire, animals, and the elements), keeping strategic reserves (to alleviate crop failures), and maintaining prices. All major cities of the Spanish Empire had an *alhóndiga*, a public granary for wheat and maize storage. Until the nineteenth century, Barcelona's municipal authorities oversaw granaries, milling, and bread production and distribution, selling it at fixed prices; they also employed bakers and oven tenders. For urban dwellers, bakeries were where food policies materialized in the price and quality of bread (Pérez Samper, 2002).

By the early twentieth century, alhóndigas were mere symbols of a bygone era, which fin de siècle cities sought to eradicate; they did so, most notably, with the reconstruction and beautification of public markets – large buildings with stained-glass windows, ample corridors, and tile stands. In Northern and Mediterranean Europe, the Americas, and Asia, urban food supply modernization followed different paths. In single-market cities like London, residents made long trips to purchase foodstuffs at its central halls and visited neighborhoods' open-air markets. By contrast, Paris, Barcelona, and Mexico City had multiple markets ranging across the urban sprawl. With three million inhabitants circa 1890, Paris had a wider variety of food retailing system compared to New York and London. The Parisian food provision network relied on multiple actors, including rural producers, who sold goods at Les Grandes Halles – retailers, greengrocers, and street vendors in almost every *quartier*, which required an enormous bureaucracy to function. Hundreds of technicians, veterinary surgeons, bacteriologists, municipal hygienists, inspectors of weights and measures, and police officers administered and supervised these traders' businesses (Sullivan, 1913). Following this example, Madrid established a market police force in 1905.

Innovation and tradition characterized municipal authorities' modernization efforts of public markets. In the 1880s, Mexico City counted six such marketplaces where authorities hoped all vendors would sell their fresh products, meats, and grains, thus facilitating oversight of the quality, price, and weight of perishables. But residents continued to offer produce they might have harvested in their backyards at the city's central plaza (Zócalo) and outside the walls of public markets (Bleynat, 2021: 17). Beyond the delivery of those goods, wholesalers from the hinterland passed through the Texcoco and Chalco Canals bringing fruits and vegetables to the city. However, "Lagoon pirates" (as the press dubbed hoarders) occasionally imposed their rule by stockpiling staples. In the summer of 1881, Mexico City once again confronted flour and coal shortages (which jeopardized bread production). The local press suggested that city council resort to a colonial practice – baking bread in ovens at the national prison to sell it at cost.[1]

Although the hygiene movement sought to establish rigid separation between city and country – isolating corrals and hatcheries from urban areas – produce from urban gardens was sold and consumed in markets, streets, and homes. Globally, in times of scarcity, some municipalities promoted intracity food provision. Relief gardens in Detroit and other metropolises in the United States during the 1890s crisis and traditional garden plots or dachas in urban Russia (Zavisca, 2003) somewhat allowed the poor to experience land ownership and agency over their well-being and eating.

In the cities of Eastern Asia, the urban food marketing panorama was different, and municipal markets were a new undertaking. In 1893, the Shanghai International Settlement opened the Shanghai HongKew Market; although in Chinese cities like Suzhou, centralization was difficult given vendors' resistance to moving their operations inside markets, other cities followed suit, hoping to improve hygiene, control prices, and increase revenue (Wang, 2022). In 1918, Tokyo and Osaka implemented their first municipally controlled markets; and later Nagoya, Kyoto, and Kobe (Harada, 2016). Until then, governors oversaw wholesale markets where peddlers acquired goods they sold in the streets (see Figure 1).

Beyond centralizing food distribution and facilitating government scrutiny, public markets were socializing spaces where the poor and middle class, mostly women, interacted. Patrons who wandered the halls of fin de siècle markets marveled at wholly modern refrigeration and lighting technologies, drinking water and sewage infrastructures. They also encountered novel food preservation and packaging methods and grappled with new weights and measures systems and health inspections of animals and perishables. Despite these advances, a leading Mexico City newspaper described public markets as "centers of all evil . . . and filthy."[2]

Before the expansion of refrigeration technologies, the permanent danger of disease – like typhus, tuberculosis, yellow fever, and diphtheria – and food deterioration threatened cities and their citizens; local governments sought to combat these ills via sanitary interventions. The London City Council was foremost concerned with fresh meat and fish sales. Between 1855 and 1870, the city built the Metropolitan Cattle Market in Islington to process live animals. The old Smithfield Market, where animals from South America and the United States had arrived for years (alongside chickens and game), was renovated to trade meat. In the city's working-class neighborhoods, small groceries, butcheries, and food

---

[1] *El Monitor Republicano* (Mexico City), July 30, 1881; August 10, 1881.
[2] "Los mercados son centros de todo mal," *Excelsior*, July 9, 1922.

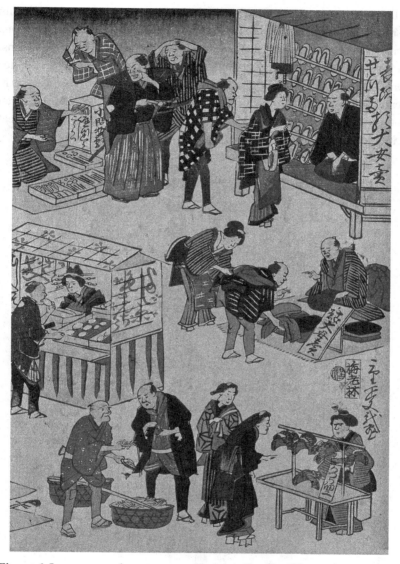

Figure 1 Japanese market scene: vendors are shown selling combs and hair ornaments, sandals, cloth, rice paste cakes and wigs. Color woodcut by Shigenobu, 1865.

Source: Wellcome Collection. Public Domain Mark.

carts sold fruits and vegetables; day and night, open-air markets offered food-stuffs to dwellers. But even as such open-air markets delivered essential food-stuffs for working- and middle-class Londoners, local authorities believed they posed risks to urban hygiene and food safety (Kelley, 2016). Circa 1910, the

Berlin government controlled fresh fish sales, hoping to supply healthy and affordable goods for the waged poor (Sullivan, 1913: 198–99). The Barcelona municipality regulated twelve marketplaces, as well as butcher shops, cattle pens, and urban gardens. In 1891, the city established a new municipal service for animal health inspection at the slaughterhouse. A few years later, veterinarians in Buenos Aires, Montevideo, and La Plata – from where British and American meatpacking companies (*frigoríficos*) exported frozen meat and the Liebig's meat extract (see Figure 2) – instituted similar services.

Figure 2 Véritable Extrait de viande (Real Meat Extract), author unidentified, France, 1890.

Source: Gallica, Bibliothèque National de France.

Slaughterhouses were of particular interest to local governments as they attempted to supply plenty of safe meat to urban workers while hiding animals from public view. City officials approached the binary supply/sanitary problem in the following manner: cattle slaughtering and fresh meat retailing in acceptable hygienic conditions had to be conducted in a geographically circumscribed area during the first hours of the day (after which meat was supposed to be salted because it was no longer deemed edible). It is not surprising that the slaughter-house would be near a highly populated area at the city center, which also facilitated inspection by local officials. These animals were fattened relatively nearby and walked on the hoof to municipal slaughterhouses. In the United States, meatpacking disrupted such arrangements, for animals raised afar and abroad could arrive in cities, where industrial plants quickly transformed herds into meat and distributed to multiple localities across the country – and beyond. Small butchers who could not compete with affordable meat practically disappeared from the provision chain. Knowing that these innovations threatened their liveli-hood, small butchers and municipal authorities in Mexico City, Paris, and Rio de Janeiro engaged in open resistance against the meat industry. They concurred that the best way to provide essential food to residents was to leave it at the local level of governance, opting for maintaining the municipal monopoly over meat distri-bution – abattoir system. No other foodstuff illustrates more vividly the tension between local and transnational forces.

The conflict between opposing forces and interests was made vivid in street vending operations. In London and New York, retailers lobbied to eliminate this type of trade; nonetheless, on occasions, they favored open-air retail because it attracted foot traffic. Street selling of prepared food or food cooked in streets required complex planning. The seller had to keep the dish warm, invest in fuel (charcoal or coal), arrange the transportation of makeshift kitchens and other gadgets, and secure a vending location. In the 1880s, Mexican tamaleras adhered to these very strictures in the urban United States. In the early 1900s, public hygiene works transformed Los Angeles's and San Antonio's Spanish cityscapes, eliminating tamale carts and chili and enchilada stands tended by Mexican migrants from their streets and plazas (Pilcher, 2012). Such mandates of good governance and hygiene, which were meant to promote prosperity and sanitation, social order, and peace, reveal deep inequalities concerning the right to occupy what spaces in cities. In Mexico City, the prospects of female food vendors (*vendedoras*) were no better; urban sanitation administrators confis-cated their stalls and labeled their activities public nuisances. Mexico's shift into modernity called for ending old customs (including street vending) that blurred the line between public and private spaces and imperiled public order. Vendedoras questioned such assertions in multiple petitions to Mexico City's government, defending their right to work in the thoroughfares and street corners as an "honorable" way to support their children (Porter, 2003: 134).

It would be a mistake to frame the social hygiene thinking and intervention programs as top-down projects. Socialist organizations shared these principles – although seeking different outcomes – and actively created cooperatives to offer all necessities to their membership, from food to fuel and housing. The cooperative movement was also a driving force behind allotment gardens in Berlin, London, and Paris. Unions and socialist parties promoted workers' self-reliance and mutualism to resist exploitation; nothing was more liberating than cultivating one's food (Nilsen, 2014: 27–28). In Buenos Aires, such organizations supported open-air markets and other consumer cooperative or mutualist organizations. The consumer cooperative *La Internacional*, founded by the *Centro Socialista de Talleres*, offered "food items and other essentials in a condition of complete purity and at the lowest [price] possible."[3] Other cooperatives carried tea, rice, Brazilian coffee, olive oil, starch, kerosene, soap, and candles. Through co-ops, these class-based organizations sought to establish direct supplies, bypassing middlemen whom workers, middle-class consumers, and governments often identified as the "visible hands of the market" (Lluch, 2015: n.p.) and blamed for shortages, high prices, and other market irregularities.

Cooperatives also prescribed the items to which workers and their families should have access to realize adequate living standards – later known as social security. Some employers also bet on recreation areas and allotments in industrial villages to counter miserable housing and working conditions, securing ambiguous achievements. At the turn of the twentieth century, women employed in Tokyo's and Osaka's spinning mills lived in companies' quarters – wooden shack dormitories for two dozen coworkers – and enjoyed three daily meals "consisting of rice and fish."[4] Although these laborers had their housing and alimentary needs met, they endured an eleven-hour working day and were subject to strict discipline. A news article from 1900 describes them as "pale and tired ... women, men, and children [who] worked day and night, in frantic and noisy workshops." Not only were these factories insalubrious spaces but the cities in which they were located were also filthy. Likening Japanese cities to any big, industrial metropolis in Europe, the piece depicts Osaka's skyline as smoke-darken by a "forest of chimneys."[5]

---

[3] *La Vanguardia* (Buenos Aires), November 12, 1915; June 2, 1900; April 6, 1906; January 10, 1915.

[4] "A questão operaria e o pauperismo no Japão," *Gazeta de Notícias* (Rio de Janeiro), February 5, 1900.

[5] Ibid.

The global hygienist agenda fueled anxieties around gender; as more women joined the urban labor force, apprehensions over their social standing and reproductive health escalated. Mutualist organizations, political parties, physicians, and feminist associations agreed that urban working and living conditions threatened families and their cities' demographic trends. In New York City, concerns arose about how to feed working women in the city, a subject pronounced upon by a 1905-newspaper article titled "The Feeding of New York's Downtown Women Workers – A New Social Phenomenon."[6] In the late nineteenth century, restaurants in several US cities reserved dining areas for unescorted women. The "Ladies' Lunch Rooms" and "Ladies' Lunch Counter" were not without precedent; since the mid-1800s, high-end eateries in the United States had rooms for unaccompanied "respectable women." The "new social phenomenon" was the massive female presence in clerical and retail jobs in cities nationwide. Victorian gender ideals dictated that men should accompany women outside their homes; hence, typists, receptionists, bookkeepers, and those employed in retail and service positions had few options about where to enjoy their midday meals. Aside from challenging gender norms, "Feeding the working girl" – as the title of another article proclaimed – was a pressing issue because of women's low wages. New York and Chicago philanthropic associations established "noonday rest and lunch clubs" to offer cheaper food exclusively for their female membership. Of course, these articles concern a specific sector of the urban worker – white, middle-class, or professional women who, as opposed to factory workers or street vendors, had a "right" to privacy. While these sources reveal the inadequacy of gendered social norms in the face of economic transformation, they also expose the underpinnings of urban trouble: the appropriate way to feed wage laborers working under strict schedules and discipline away from their homes.

Improving Workers' Diets

Feeding healthy citizens was a sociobiological component of municipal governance. Chief on the urban agenda was the need to curb food deprivation, "immoderate" working-class drinking, and infant mortality. To this end, specific measurements of the kind, quality, and quantity of foodstuffs needed for working-class families to thrive became standard in political discourses across cities. Data provided scientific backing and a benchmark against which the eating habits in different cities were gauged. Studies in Chicago (1895), New York (1896), Tokyo (1898), Santiago de Chile (1907), Mexico City (1909), Buenos Aires (1907), and

---

[6] "The Feeding of New York's Down Town Women Workers – A New Social Phenomenon," *The New York Times*, October 15, 1905.

Bombay (1916–25) concluded that working-class individuals spent 50 percent of their wages on food. Others saw alcoholism and correlated "vices" as signs of inadequate eating and "race degeneration." Medical doctors, sanitarians, municipal officials, teachers, and philanthropic organizations embarked on missions to educate the public on the benefits of "rational dieting," especially in capital cities. As they used extant scientific knowledge to shape the consumption habits of urban populations, discourses favorable to rational dieting became intertwined with notions of bodily and material success. Individuals who partook in protein-rich foodstuffs were healthier and wealthier than their counterparts who did not, and so were their nations. Indeed, governments, nutritionists, and public officials came to promote meat as healthy and nutritious (See Figure 3) (Neill, 2009). Such ideals challenged even the Japanese traditional plant-based diet. By the 1870s, Tokyo's and Osaka's residents were regularly eating beef pot (*gyūnabe*) seasoned with miso or soy sauce (Mitsuda, 2023: 10). In the mid-1800s, technical innovations in the animal, meat, and dairy industries (and a good dose of political will) made it possible to extend the carnivorous diet to a broad spectrum of the poor.

Meat consumption trends accelerated in cities of meat-exporting economies in the early twentieth century. In 1913 Montevideo, a childless working-class couple could partake of five hundred grams of meat and ¾ liters of milk daily. One year later, the Uruguayan Ministry of Labor boasted that whereas a skilled laborer in Montevideo worked sixteen minutes to buy one kilo of meat, "in France," the ratio was four times higher (Barrán & Nahum, 1984: 28). In Buenos Aires, from 1914 to 1923, annual apparent consumption of beef and mutton was about 101 to 130 kilos per capita (Lluch, 2015: 120). In the late nineteenth century, cities where fresh mutton or beef was part of dwellers' diets, such as London, saw increased consumption and substitution of traditional animal foods for new ones. In the first decades of the 1900s, salaried workers in New York City, for instance, ate more beef cattle than the customary salt pork. In Rio de Janeiro, renovation of the city's central slaughterhouse made fresh beef plentiful to the point that it eventually replaced salted meat in the urban market. An analogous phenomenon occurred in 1920s Barcelona, as the working class incorporated more beef, lamb, goat, and pork meat into their meals, they ate less salted cod, and old source of animal protein.

Nevertheless, meat access remained unequal across the urban working class worldwide. In cities of Central and Eastern Europe, workers continued to rely on traditional sources of animal protein, sausages, together with potatoes and bread. In Moscow, "pork sausage [was] one of the few foods besides bread that a poor worker could have in a hurry" (Masterovoy, 2013: 13). In 1939, far away in Bogotá, despite

Figure 3 Ármese con hierro para combatir la anemia. 200 gramos de carne contienen 7 miligramos de hierro (Arm Yourself with Iron to Fight Anemia. 200 Grams of Meat Contain 7 Milligrams of Iron).

Source: *Servir. Revista de la Escuela de Estudios Argentinos*, Buenos Aires, June 12, 1936; Centro de Documentación e Investigación de la Cultura de Izquierdas (CEDINCI), Buenos Aires.

the local government's expectations, Colombian physicians attested with alarm that workers did not partake in fraction "of the meat necessary ... to be healthy, robust, ... and prosperous" (qtd. in Pohl-Valero, 2016: 127).

Alongside meat, scientific consensus about fresh milk's health properties made it the central beverage of public policies; medical doctors recommended its daily consumption, especially by the poor and children for good nutrition. Campaigns to promote milk intake emerged everywhere. In Latin American capitals of the 1920s, public schools offered milk rations to children. In crowded working-class neighborhoods, milk depots (*gotas de leche*) offered mothers and infants with fresh milk rations and breast milk substitutes. Gotas de leche – public, philanthropic, or mutualist – were designed to improve the health and life expectancy of urban populations by changing children's material and biological traits. On the one hand, milk stations were instruments of public health campaigns mandating milk pasteurization; on the other, they functioned as rational motherhood laboratories. At milk depots, mothers were instructed on how to provide healthy food to children and take care of them.

However, accepting pasteurization as a public policy to provide cheap milk to the poor was not straightforward. In 1908, Chicago promulgated the first municipal pasteurization law in the United States, but city officials and interest groups continued to favor other hygiene practices (production control, inspection, and bacterial counts). Such ambivalence led to an eight-year delay in implementing full pasteurization. Contesting views – within the political and medical sectors – and suspicions over industrialization and technology, as the example of Chicago shows, were widespread (Czaplicki, 2007).

Additionally, municipalities encountered myriad difficulties regulating and commercializing fresh milk. In late nineteenth-century Havana, milk sellers herded cows across town, retailing the liquid in public plazas and in front of dwellers' doors – a task they performed swiftly, for fresh milk under "the sun's heat . . . [soured] quickly or turned into butter" (Sarmiento Ramírez, 2002: 223–24). In Buenos Aires, pasteurized milk "competed with raw milk sold by milkmen . . . who bought it directly from dairy farmers" (Knecher & Fuld, 1998: 165). In 1892, as the city continued to face sanitary challenges and milk adulteration (watering), local officials banned the transit of cows in city streets. They promised to install "model dairy farms in Buenos Aires's surroundings, to supply milk in hygienic and clean conditions" (qtd. in Gómez & Zubizarreta, 2015: 88). In Barcelona in the first half of the twentieth century, authorities sponsored campaigns to promote milk as a healthy food. The Catalonian government drafted regulations on milk retailing, established agencies to oversee its quality, and provided the beverage in school lunch programs. For their part, milk companies pasteurized, bottled the product, and distributed it to consumers' doors. Between 1900 and 1933, milk consumption in Barcelona rose by 500 percent, more than any other animal-derived food (Adell & Pujol, 2017: 66).

Milk consumption was not prevalent in urban Asia in the early twentieth century. In China's port cities, milk was marginal, linked to the elderly and infant diets. As the beverage became increasingly associated with the modern diet, scientists, intellectuals, and nutritionists sought to extend its consumption. Looking for a substitute attuned to Chinese environmental conditions, they found it in *doujiang*, a tofu ingredient – later recast as soybean milk. Although cities like Harbin, Beijing, and Shanghai had dairy industries, milk prices and transportation costs limited widespread consumption. Soybean milk, locally produced, was affordable and as scientifically sound as cow's milk. In the 1930s, the targeted consumers were children; Shanghai and Nanjing housed institutes dedicated to studying and promoting children's welfare policies, including a diet calibrated to their physical constitution. Nanjing, for instance, sponsored a program to allocate soybean milk to children to combat malnutrition. Private companies began promoting soybean milk as hygienic and modern – or, better yet, a beverage that linked contemporary scientific discoveries to classical Chinese medicine – made evident in the packaging, sterilized bottles and caps, and the language employed in the advertisements. Companies such as the Federal Soybean Milk went further, associating soybean milk drinking with progress, "Make the nation powerful and prosperous!" "Nourish and strengthen the body!" declared two campaign slogans (Fu, 2018: 117). The company made sure to distinguish its product – sold in thermoses – from doujiang, available in food stalls and tofu shops. Marketed in such a manner and distributed to family houses, this modern, healthy, and hygienic food was within reach of all (Fu, 2018).

Despite attempts by governments and business interests to extend healthy foodstuffs and nourishing beverage consumption to all sectors, these programs required time, and reached only a limited sector of the urban worker. Regular consumption of these foodstuffs was challenging, as access to refrigeration remained spotty and uneven. In 1918 Rio de Janeiro, one reader of the Carioca daily *Gazeta de Notícias* aspired to have an ice box, "The most modest worker, ... should have in his house a box with sawdust and an ice block, which would allow him to preserve his meat, fish, and the milk for his young son."[7] The implications for everyday life were considerable, unequal, and long-standing. By 1940, half of Carioca households still had no electricity.

The consumption of cereals has historically been essential to biological subsistence worldwide. Still, imperial notions of wheat's superiority over other grains accompanied its expansion (in bread form) to colonial urban tables,

---

[7] *Gazeta de Notícias* (Rio de Janeiro), September 22, 1918.

portraying it as inherently wholesome. In the late 1800s, French Equatorial Africa (*Afrique Équatoriale française*, modern Congo, Gabon, Chad, and the Central African Republic), the same doctors who studied the Parisian working-class eating habits deemed wheat more nutritious than rice, millet, maize, and sorghum (Neill, 2009). Physicians and political authorities in Rio de Janeiro and Mexico City promoted wheat in the form of sweet-and-sour bread as an alternative to native cereals, manioc meal and maize, respectively.

Since modern times, bread baking has been in the hands of professional bakers as a laborious and time-consuming undertaking; bakeries were in (almost) all corners of European and American cities. Baker's bread was affordable and energy-rich for wage laborers in Paris, London, New York, Lima, and Buenos Aires. When savored with jam or condensed milk, as enjoyed by dwellers in industrial cities in the United States and Great Britain, or with cheap meat in Buenos Aires and Montevideo, bread provided sufficient calories to sustain cash-strapped laborers and their families (Mintz, 1996; Turner, 2014). In Lima, authorities oversaw bread quality and provision as matters of hygiene and public order. They supervised all actors in the wheat supply chain, from grain importers to local producers, millers, middlemen, and bakers (Salinas Sánchez, 2013). In São Paulo, bread-making and industrial bakery transformations converged with new social habits, necessities, and expectations. In 1870, when São Paulo's population was a little over thirty thousand, small businesswomen controlled the production and door-to-door selling of maize and manioc meal bread. When industrialization and migration began to alter the city's social and economic features, bread-making moved from the domestic realm to become a full-blown artisanal (later industrial), male-dominated activity. New bakeries, a significant number owned by Italian and later Portuguese immigrants, employed men who worked night and day in specialized tasks: kneading dough by hand, attending a charcoal oven, and delivering the product across the city. Industrial wheaten bread (*pão francês*) became typical on tables in São Paulo and other Brazilian metropolises. Pão francês was not the cheapest source of carbohydrates for Paulista low-income families, but the ubiquity of bakeries made its daily consumption all but inevitable (Matos, 2009).

In many Mediterranean and American cities, another cereal, rice, was central to residents' diets. In Rio de Janeiro, rice was a typical dish in well-to-do households in the early nineteenth century. In the city's streets, freed and enslaved women sold a refreshing sweet-and-sour drink made with fermented rice and rice pudding. By the end of the century, rice consumption had become common across social strata in urban Latin America. In parts of Asia, as industrialization and urbanization took hold, polished white rice became a hallmark of urban eating for the rich – whose meals included various small dishes concluding with rice – and a staple for the poor. Once a luxury food on the continent, white rice became more accessible to urbanites at the turn of the nineteenth century. Akin to wheaten bread and meat in cities of the Americas, rice eating in Japan was driven by status. Although countryside dwellers' diets were relatively wholesome, they also sought to incorporate more rice into their meals. This dietary shift was concurrent with other material changes, such as the separation of the kitchen from other spaces in the house and purchases of kitchenware: pots, knives, plates, and – most importantly – stoves that allowed several dishes to be cooked at the same time (Francks, 2015).

Regulating Eating at Home and in the Streets

Before the eight-hour work day took hold, few wage laborers had the privilege of lunchtime. In Buenos Aires, thousands of poor European migrants worked fourteen to fifteen hours daily in the industrial, commercial, and transport sectors in the port and the city. They spent their "lunchtime" in public spaces purchasing their food from street vendors whose products dodged sanitary or bromatological regulations (Rey, 2019). Mobile kitchens brought a daily portion of chorizo and hot mate to stevedores, enabling them to withstand long and exhausting working hours at the docks. Their counterparts in La Boca neighborhood visited guesthouses (*fondas*) to buy fish and chips, Italian pasta (*fideos*), meat rolls (*matambre*), and bread and wine (Gayol, 2000: 111–33; Rey, 2019: 69–70). While some workers ate hastily on the streets, other employees worked for company towns that, by design, provided housing and services (including food).

São Paulo was another prime destination of European and Asian migrants looking for industrial work. In 1918, a factory survey revealed that most men, women, and children employed in the textile, metalwork, food, and garment sectors had one hour for lunch or dinner (according to their shift) and fifteen minutes for a coffee break. Whether those workers could afford meals in restaurants or small eateries is difficult to ascertain. If they lived near their workplaces, they probably stopped at their tenements to eat the midday meal; others might have carried lunch boxes with food prepared at home.[8] In industrial European cities, some workers walked to their homes for a warm lunch, but such an option was available to only a few. A girl in late 1880s Vienna describes her lunchtime as "a true torment. I had to walk quickly for 25 minutes, then I gulped down my hot lunch as fast as I could and rushed back to work" (qtd. in Scholliers, 1996: 245). Cooked food peddled in streets also provided sustenance

---

[8] "Inquerito às condições do trabalho em São Paulo," *Boletim do Departamento Estadual do Trabalho*, (1919). São Paulo: Typ. Brasil de Rothschild & Cia, 185–204.

for city laborers. In Mexico City, workers counted on "itinerary hawkers . . ., low eating houses" and makeshift food stands (*puestos*) where they could partake of tamales, tacos, or enchiladas (Pollard, 1913). Perhaps as a way to preserve the mid-day family meal commensality and traditional gender roles, in Orizaba (Mexico), textile workers' wives met their husbands at factory gates, bringing fresh tortillas, tamales, and other hot meals.[9] Their counterparts, along with their children, in industrial German cities did the same (Thelen, 2006). In Paris, by one account, laborers sat on park benches (see Figure 4) to lunch on a combination of fare bought from home, fried potatoes brought on the streets, and baker's bread (Bruegel, 2015).

As discussed, the early 1900s hygiene movement assumed multifaceted dimensions; promoting salubrious working and living spaces, safe food, and healthy families was paramount. In an 1886 report to São Paulo's Public Health Commission, the engineer Luiz Raphael Vieira de Souza explained how these issues intertwined: "Workers' houses improvement has not only a material aim but also a political and moral one... [a] well aired and lit room, cleaned and comfortably distributed, influences the morality and well-being of the family" (qtd. in Silva, 2014: 89). Kitchens were of particular interest to reformers who envisioned them as spaces designated exclusively to food preparation, run by women for the family's benefit. Modern kitchen appliances and devices – fueled by new energies – were vehicles of education that shaped gender roles and domesticity in capitalist and socialist cities. In its quest to build an egalitarian lifestyle, the Soviet state envisioned a household experience that was modern, efficient, and communal. In Moscow and Leningrad, houses without stoves alongside factory and collective kitchens were meant to liberate women from the household toil, allowing them to perform their public duty in the industrial sector while avoiding waste (of goods and time) intrinsic to domestic cooking (Masterovoy, 2013). But women continued to bear the brunt of domestic chores.

In the 1920s, electric and gas companies and municipal health commissions targeted urban middle classes worldwide with marketing campaigns extolling the benefits of "electric servants" and gas stoves. These adverts instructed women on the cost and comfort benefits of these technologies in their homes and the urban environment (Sharan, 2020). In Calcutta, between World Wars I and II, policies to eliminate street garbage and domestic fumes were at the

---

[9] Aurora Gómez-Galvarriato personal communication during the Inter Institutional Seminar of Economic History (SIHE, Colmex), November 2018.

Figure 4 Un qui dine mal (One who dines poorly).

Source: Goudeau, Émile (1893) *Paris qui consomme: tableaux de Paris, dessins de Pierre Vidal*, Paris, Imprimé pour Henri Beraldi, 205; Gallica, Bibliothèque National de France.

center of the colonial government's sanitary reforms.[10] British gas companies in Southern Cone capitals, like the *Compañía Primitiva de Gas* in Buenos Aires, organized public gatherings to teach young working women and housewives to cook with gas ovens, already popular in Briton cities (Rey, 2019). In São Paulo, the San Paulo Gas Company pledged that gas stoves were essential to wholesome cooking, made kitchen maids replaceable, and transformed women into "managers" of modern machinery (Silva, 2014: 92).

Historically, food preparation for most families was a household undertaking. Children and men fetched water, gathered fuelwood, tended to fires, milled flour, gridded grains, cleaned dishes, and collected trash, even in urban centers. Technological developments had a tripartite outcome of freeing men and children from most cooking-related chores, opening labor markets to women, and limiting domestic chores to the female domain (Higman, 2012), even in purportedly more equalitarian Soviet cities. Outside the urban household, other structural transformations facilitated the movements of people and goods, both once again altered the food savored in private and public spaces in the modern city as the next section investigates.

2 Transforming Urban Diets: Transoceanic Trade and Migration Flows

How did goods, commodities, and migrants converge in cities to transform urban foodways? In the late 1800s, technologies in food transport and preservation and trade agreements accelerated and diversified the exchange of goods; in cities, they modified food baskets and consumption habits. Likewise, mass migrations altered landscapes and imprinted dramatic changes to the lives of millions, reshaping public, private, communal, gender, and social relations. Numerous industrial and agro-industrial settlements arose in response to market forces and the influx of newcomers, as did mining and company towns in the northern and southern hemispheres. Fleeing misery, war, and disasters, or seeking new opportunities, rural peoples (within national and international borders) saw migration as a means to improve their quality of life. As migrants brought new ingredients and cooking expertise to cities, locals sought traditional cuisines and resisted outsiders' foodways; in the process, both were transformed. Broadly, the food experiences of newcomers in cities follow similar trends. Initially, their food is confined to ethnic neighborhoods; while this segregation reinforces a sense of community, it also facilitates the designation of native food as "inferior." Second, these

---

[10] *Report of the Indian Industrial Commission, 1915–1918*, (1919). Presented to Parliament by Command of His Majesty London, Published by his Majesty's Stationery Office, 137.

spaces become places of exotic foods and people. Finally, immigrant food-ways enter the mainstream food culture, which embraces it as national. Nonetheless, the popularity of migrant food is seldom accompanied by the visibility of workers in the food sector. Such was the situation in the early 1900s, as in the twenty-first century.

How Immigration Transformed Food and Foodways

Millions of migrants from Europe, Asia, and the Ottoman Empire arrived on the Americas' shores in the late nineteenth and early twentieth centuries. Most stayed in the United States, many settled in Latin America. From 1870 to 1914, approximately 2.5 million and two million immigrants remained in Argentina and Brazil, respectively. In Asian cities such as Shanghai and Bombay, rural national and international migrants sought employment in factories, retail, finance, and infrastructure works. Agricultural expansion, industrialization, and government programs seeking to broaden the labor force for fields and factories spurred these formidable transnational popula-tion movements. Domestically, commercial farming and increased competi-tion for land pushed landless peasants to relocate to fast-growing industrial and mining cities, like Antofagasta, Tarapacá, and Iquique in northern Chile. Internal labor migration in Peru also accounted for significant demographic changes in Lima; in 1908, almost 60 percent of its population was born outside the city (Klarén, 1986: 614). In the United States, after the Civil War (1861–65), millions of African Americans fled the South to work in industrial facilities in the North. The pace of migration increased in the latter decades of the nineteenth century and accelerated around World War I. Between 1910 and 1920, the African American population in New York rose from 90,000 to 150,000; in Chicago from 44,000 to 109,000; and in Detroit from 5,000 to 40,000 (Grossman, 1989: 4). Together, these "translocal" migrations – a term used here to denote labor flows across and within nations – stimulated demographic growth and diversity in cities and brought rural foodways to the fore of the urban dining experience.

Worldwide, at the beginning of the twentieth century, in every major city, national and foreign-born male and female migrants worked in the food-processing sector (in dairy, meatpacking, and brewer companies), in restaurants and households (as cooks, waiters, housekeepers, and bakers), and public spaces as peddlers of fruits, vegetables, and prepared food. They also estab-lished groceries and lunch counters catering primarily but not exclusively to their community members. In 1919, the Angeleno newspaper *La Prensa* (pub-lished in Spanish) printed ads from the "Liberty Meat Market" – a Chinese meat market that offered "fresh beef, pork, and mutton meat . . ., and *cecina*," a salt-cured, dried meat, and staple of Mexican cuisine.[11] In Mexico City during the 1910 Revolution, displacements and migrations, coupled with food scarcity, increased demand for prepared foods in inns, guest houses, and popular kitchens tended by poor migrant women whose male relatives were in the battlefield (Zenteno Roldán, 2014: 77–78). In Barcelona, migrants from other Mediterranean cities of Italian and French origin set up bourgeois restaurants and traditional inns.

The diffusion of ramen in Japan is emblematic of how migrant foodways evolved, adapting to novel consumption contexts. In the 1880s, Chinese cooks introduced this noodle soup to the island country; they were employed at restaurants catering almost exclusively to their fellow nationals working and trading in the port cities of Yokohama, Kobe, Kawasaki, and Hakodate. Three or four decades later, Chinese restaurants spread (as the Japanese government permitted foreigners to leave designated neighborhoods) while their cooks found employment in Japanese eateries. As they did, the dish evolved with added ingredients (soy sauce, for example) and integrated into the eating habits of workers, soldiers, and students. By the 1920s, ramen was already typical fare in Japanese cities. Such developments coincided with Japan's industrial push and imperial preeminence after the First Sino-Japanese War (1894–95). The government incentivized wheat cultivation (for noodle production) in the colonies while a hungry mass of workers arrived in cities. By then, urban consumers could find ramen – a hearty and affordable fast food – almost everywhere, in restaurants and eateries (Chinese- or Japanese-owned and Western) and street pushcarts (Solt, 2014). The global spreading of shawarma – a Middle Eastern dish consisting of meat cooked on a vertical spit accompanied by flat bread demonstrates the hybridization process migrant foods spurred. Brought to Brazilian and Mexican cities by Middle Eastern immigrants in the early twentieth century, shawarma become an urban street food in both countries, with remarkable differences. In Mexico, "taco al pastor" uses pork meat seasoned with chiles and is savored with tortillas; in Brazil, "churrasco grego" consists of beef, eaten with wheat bread.

Consider the expansion of Chinese food in US cities. Chinese urban labor was already active on the East Coast in the mid-1800s; in the West, it followed migration waves after the US-Mexican War (1846–48). Chinese eateries, as well as butcher shops and grocery stores that sold essential Asian ingredients, became ubiquitous in Sacramento and San Francisco. These restaurants were

---

[11] *La Prensa* (Los Angeles), July 5, 1919.

usually located in segregated areas and catered almost exclusively to working-class, single migrant men. In this first phase, immigrant food and ingredients were deemed low, dirty, and essentially different from "national" cuisines. In the 1880s, Chinese Americans increased their presence in Chicago and Boston, as did their eateries and food businesses. Concurrently, ethnic neighborhoods caught tourists' attention (Chen, 2017). In 1907, the *Los Angeles Herald* printed an article praising the district's opening to outsiders. Still, it warned the potential visitor not to be alarmed by its untidy streets, "for there exists no contagious diseases . . . no one has ever been known to contract any disease from association in the district." As for its food, the piece continues, "Chinatown is not Chinatown unless there is plenty of dirt and grease."[12] From such descriptions, Chinese restaurants and foods left ethnic neighborhoods to become Chinese American.

Chinese workers arrived in Peru as indentured servants just after the abolition of slavery in the mid-1800s. They mainly settled on coastal sugarcane and cotton plantations and railroad construction sites, where precarious conditions compelled them to cook for their community members, using native ingredients while preserving their cooking methods. In the 1870s, after indentured servitude ended, Peruvian-born Chinese, alongside free Chinese nationals, moved to Trujillo, Lima, and Callao. Most worked in the retail sector; others established eateries that catered to the urban working class. In Lima, the elite sought in-house Chinese cooks as a sign of affluence; the role of these workers was multidirectional; while adapting their cuisine to local ingredients and employers' tastes, they also influenced the household menu (Yuan, 2018).

Despite the popularity of Chinese food in Peru's leading cities on the Pacific coast, ambivalence toward Chinese arrivals and their foodways was apparent in discourse and practice. In the early 1900s, although immigration from China had significantly diminished, the Peruvian press openly express a belief that this population would "degenerate" the Peruvian "race." Concurrently, other publications labeled their food diseased and unhygienic. These accusations reached a zenith in 1909, when Chinese neighborhoods and businesses in Lima were demolished and ransacked. In 1908, about 40 percent of Chinese immigrants in Lima worked in the commercial sector of this capital (Villafuerte, 2012: 131). While a small group owned retail houses linked to Hong Kong businesses – which facilitated imports of Asian foods and ingredients – the number of fondas grew. As Chinese foodstuffs and spices became readily available, cooks innovated preparing criollo dishes using Asian cutting techniques (horizontal slicing) and cooking methods (stir-frying).[13] By the

---

[12] "Chinese Prepare for Fiesta Week," *Los Angeles Herald*, April 21, 1907.
[13] *El Comercio* (Lima), January 9, 1909; *El Peruano* (Lima), July 26, 1921.

1930s, the word *chifa* had entered the lexicon of Peruvians, used today to describe restaurants that serve Chinese Peruvian food and the fare cooked in these eateries. Multicultural hybrids, like chifa, illustrate the conjunction of local and global trends at urban tables.

Migrants arriving in nineteenth-century Buenos Aires adopted the local diet regardless of their origin; they brought with them Eurasian eating habits but cherished the local red meat, particularly beef, thanks to its abundance, accessibility, and easy preparation. Wheat and wheat flour were also plentiful; as a result, Italian pasta production and consumption spread across communities of different ethnicities, classes, and national origins. In 1892, Buenos Aires alone had forty pasta factories. These plants' daily output amounted to 120,000 kilograms of spaghetti; yearly, the Buenos Aires-Rosario urban axis consumed thirty-six thousand metric tons of fideos (Helguera, 1893: 4, 39). By contrast, in London, the colonial cuisine from the British dominions of South Asia remained ethnically segregated until the nineteenth century. This cuisine evolved in the kitchens of urban and rural British homes and clubs in India, Pakistan, Malaysia, and Singapore. In these spaces, while Chinese Hainanese cooks adapted Asian foods to their employers' tastes, British officials and cookbook authors disseminated colonial cookery in London. They brought curry variants and nutritious, simple foods for children and the sick, such as pishpash (rice porridge cooked with small pieces of meat). Soon after, London menus offered versions of these dishes for the average Briton consumer (Leong-Salobir, 2015).

How Market Forces Transformed Food and Foodways

According to a paper that John McCall (agent-general for Tasmania for the British Empire) read before the Royal Society for the Encouragement of Arts, Manufactures and Commerce in 1910, "Apples can be placed in London from countries thousands of miles away at a lower cost than they can be brought by rail from the fruit-growing districts of England to the great consuming and distributing center at the heart of the Empire – the City of London" (McCall, 1910).[14] Behind this statement lie a host of issues, including complex trade networks and imperial economic projects. Geographic conditions were also significant. Opposing seasons for fruits and vegetables in the northern and southern hemispheres allowed apples produced in Tasmania or grapes and pineapple in South Africa to be delivered in England "at a time when fresh fruit is scarce."[15] British ports imported and re-exported tea from India, salted

---

[14] "Fruit Production of the British Empire," *Journal of the Royal Society of Arts 58* (2992), 475–485: 480.
[15] Ibid., 477.

and dried fruits from Persia, and salt from Calcutta mills, which Liverpool factories processed. The United Kingdom also brought in staples: wheat from India, South America, central Europe, and Russia, and meat, cheese, butter, and cream from pastoral economies worldwide.

Urban European grocers carried tropical products – coffee, spices, sugar, vanilla, or cinnamon-infused chocolates – for centuries. Nonetheless, until the mid-nineteenth century, bananas, citrus, pineapple, and other tropical goods (coconuts, mangoes, avocados) were luxury items, rarely present on North Atlantic tables and recipes, perhaps except for Andalusia's cuisine. The transport revolution of the 1850s sharply reduced freight rates and facilitated goods' exchange across oceans. Improvements in wholesale and retail and renewed infrastructure allowed for the availability of such diverse fruits to the European urban consumer. In Berlin, new department stores provided a vast supply of ultramarine goods (including fresh and dry fruits and produce) to restaurants, public kitchens, and bakeries, all individually packaged and priced. Big retail and street food presented their goods to consumers differently, even as they complemented each other. In the 1870s, Berlin's city council prohibited food street sales; two decades later, the municipality opted to control rather than ban such trade, which allowed poor children to access fruits from South America and Southern Europe, like oranges and the nutritious banana (Sullivan, 1913).

For urban consumers in the Northern Hemisphere, bananas were "the king" of tropical fruits. European cities have received regular provisions of bananas from Portuguese islands, African colonies, and the Canary Islands since the early modern era. During the nineteenth century, British and French merchants organized a banana trade from the Caribbean to Europe (Reynolds, 2003: 27), Jamaica being the primary supplier to British cities (Fawcett, 1921). Since the mid-1800s, bananas and other tropical fruits arrived in US cities from plantations in Hawaii, Mexico, the Caribbean, and Central and South America. By the late nineteenth century Standard Fruit Company and United Fruit Company controlled such trade. Initially, bananas were exclusive to the tables of well-to-do in exotic desserts; in the early 1900s, their consumption spread among urban laborers for its low-price, high-calorie content, and easy-to-store properties.[16] As early morning meals in the United States shifted from fats and proteins to cereal and bread, bananas were a wholesome addition. In 1900, those companies sold almost twenty million bunches of bananas worldwide; thirteen years later, they poured twice as many bananas into the global market (Striffler & Moberg, 2003: 4).

---

[16] "The Banana," *The New York Times*, March 16, 1902.

Even in cold Stockholm, where the first shipment of Banana Company AB to Gothenburg arrived frozen (barely making its way to markets) and consumers were unfamiliar with the fruit (they did not know how to eat it), banana consumption spread rapidly and enthusiastically among urban residents. In the early 1900s, leftist parliamentarians attuned to Stockholm dwellers' fondness for their summer banana snacks lobbied to eliminate taxes and duties on the tropical fruit. Like the debate around milk in other urban centers, "the banana discourse" in Sweden advertised the fruit as highly nutritious, easily digestible, and hygienic (Guerrero Cantarell, 2019: 20). Other European consumers demonstrated a similar palate for bananas. In Marseille and Rome, consumption of bananas imported from African colonies increased during the interwar period. In Genoa, Trieste, and Milan, Italian housewives purchased the fruit at "La Casa della Banana" kiosks (Garvin, 2023).

Over the past four centuries, few tropical goods have had more relevance to urban foodways and imperial endeavors than sugar, tea, and coffee, all of which arrived in European capital cities as exotic delicacies and eventually came to be mass consumption goods. Sugar evolved from a medicine to a luxury item to a staple in working-class diets thanks to dramatic changes in agricultural production and slave labor. In nineteenth-century imperial cities, sugar became an essential source of calories for workers and a symbol of upward mobility in London, Paris, Amsterdam, Marseille, and other industrial hubs (Mintz, 1996). The spread of coffee consumption was genuinely global, reaching multiple regions via different streams – even more so than tea, a hot Asian drink introduced (with sugar) to Western tables in the eighteenth century (Sanghera, 2023). From its origins in Africa and the Islamic world, Arab groups introduced coffee to Granada, the center of Al Andalus (the Muslim Empire that ruled large swaths of the Iberian Peninsula from the eighth to the fifteenth centuries). In the 1500s, coffee landed in Europe at the hands of Italian merchants. Later, coffee beans from India, Ceylon, Java, Madagascar, and Jamaica arrived in Amsterdam, and the main ports of England and France; soon after, in coffeehouses in Lisbon, Madrid, Cadiz, Barcelona, Venice, Paris, and London (Dufour, 1671). Spanish and Portuguese empires brought coffee and sugar to their American domains, as did French and British colonizers in Haiti, Martinique, Saint-Domingue, and Jamaica. Two technological innovations facilitated the mass consumption of coffee in the late nineteenth century: the amelioration of bean roasting "torrefaction" and its mechanized preparation.[17] Coffee brewed in Italian espresso machines – the first dating from the early

---

[17] *Le café: une révolution dans ses procédés de torréfaction, par L'Ingénieur Le Turcq Des Rosiers*, (1890), Paris, Publications de la Société Française d'Hygiène, Georges Carré Éditeur.

twentieth century – became, if not the norm, the aspiration of coffeehouses worldwide.

In Istanbul, the Turkish metropolis, cafés for merchants, religious figures, and wealthy men, and coffee street selling for the common folk have at least five centuries of history. In European cities, Paris among others, coffee drinking was and remained connected to sociability and intellectual and political discussion, even clandestine planning, since the French Revolution (Rude, 1877). In 1800 Buenos Aires, cafés spread all over the city, adopting ethnic names: *Café de los Catalanes* and, later, *Café Turco*. As the city grew, so did coffee consumption among the working class, who enjoyed coffee and hot mate in the streets, coffeehouses, and at home (Gayol, 2000). In households, they likely brew ground beans – predominantly marketed in cans – of Brazilian, Cuban, or Javan origins, as extensive press adverts reveal.[18]

Surrounded by coffee plantations, Havana saw its first coffeehouses in the mid-1700s. In the nineteenth century, thanks to the coffee export business, roasting houses offering ground beans and prepared coffee prospered. Coffee drinking was a daily habit that crossed racial and social boundaries in Havana and other Caribbean cities like San Juan de Puerto Rico. Cities in the United States consumed Brazilian, Mexican, and Caribbean coffee. In the early 1900s, George C. L. Washington, a Belgian who settled in the United States, developed an instant coffee variety that became a staple in Europe during World War I; in the interwar years, the G. Washington Coffee Company massively advertised its product on the airwaves and in newspapers (Schoenholt, 2018: 36–37). Urban bakeries across the United States also sold ready-to-eat, inexpensive meals with pastries and coffee.[19] As one expected, in Belle Époque Paris, coffee was an essential hot beverage whose consumption traversed social and economic boundaries: "cafe avec petite verre" was on menus of both working-class eateries and high-end restaurants (Bruegel, 2015: 275). Even in tea-drinking London, busy passersby could savor a cup of coffee in multiple stalls located across the city.

Until the mid-twentieth century, the bulk of beans in global markets origin-ated in Brazil's southeast plantations (having displaced Asian farms). In the early 1800s in Rio de Janeiro, the elites drank coffee as a habit; by the midcentury, its consumption began to spread to the working class. In the city, physicians associated coffee with intellectual endeavors; hence, they praised such changes, framing coffee as a "hygiene modifier," a beverage for the

---

[18] *La Vanguardia* (Buenos Aires), August 28, 1897.

[19] New York Public Library, "What Is on the Menu?" Huether & Steffens. Vienna Bakery and Lunchroom, September 1, 1917. [online] http://menus.nypl.org/menu_pages/67976/, (accessed June 20, 2020).

"civilized man" (Couto & Alfonso-Goldfarb, 2016: 44; Turner, 2014). Coffee drinking was common after meals for its digestive properties. Later, it became a morning beverage, a stimulant to start the working day. In hand with São Paulo's urban and industrial growth, tea drinking diminished as coffee became less expensive. In the 1920s, Paulista coffeehouses catered to upper-class individuals who gathered to read newspapers and discuss daily affairs, while neighborhood bars sold *cafezinho* to working-class folks. In San José and Heredia (Costa Rica), a coffee-exporting region since the mid-nineteenth century, inhabitants drank coffee in a jar or gourd accompanied by biscuits, tamales, and local dishes. In early 1900s Costa Rica, city cafés as conviviality centers thrived, although they remained socially segregated. The affluent patronized European-style coffeehouses, while the urban poor frequented *cafés josefinos*, inns in which, after the 1910s, women served coffee with tamales and bread with eggs (Vega Jiménez, 2002: 103, 108). Gender and class divisions also shaped coffee drinking in Colombian cities. Visited predominantly by men, coffee houses in provincial capital cities forged identities based on patrons' social standing: livestock owners and cowhands, coffee plantation landlords and workers, university students, urban laborers, and settlers in the peripheries each frequented their own cafés (Tocancipá-Falla, 2006).

Despite extensive evidence that coffee consumption crossed social lines, North Atlantic–centered descriptions maintain that "poor countries have grown coffee for rich ones" (Clarence-Smith & Topik, 2003: 2). The Global South harvested and processed coffee. It also extensively drank coffee across race and class boundaries, in town and country alike. Urban sanitation and hygiene movements finally reinforced coffee drinking at home, the workplace, and in the streets, greatly broadening its consumption. Worldwide temperance organizations sought to counter alcoholism by incentivizing coffee drinking among the urban working poor, establishing coffee shops and restaurants as alternatives to bars. In Liverpool, the Workers Club site had "a restaurant and café, meeting and reading rooms, a library, an economy kitchen, a garden with games and gym exercises."[20] Other temperance coffeehouses served meals and hot beverages, including chocolate – as was the case in 1920s Mexico City, a city immersed in profound social changes after the 1910 Revolution. Municipal and national media campaigns against *pulque*[21] – an agave-fermented drink primarily associated with rural Mexico – and *pulquerías*

---

[20] "Sciencia para todos. A luta contra o alcolismo. O tratamento seroterapico do cancro," *Gazeta de Notícias* (Rio de Janeiro), January 13, 1901.

[21] "Pulque in Mexico, Now in Official Disfavor, Has a Place among National Beverages," *The New York Times*, January 20, 1935.

increased workers' consumption of coffee and other industrial beverages, including sodas (Orange Crush) and beer (Ramírez Rodríguez, 2015).

The urban needs of cities immersed in such demographic and social changes birthed yet another novelty: takeout food. Inns, restaurants, and cafeterias in train and tram stations and ports began offering affordable food for quick eating to migrants, travelers, workers, and other commuters. Despite apprehensions about hygiene, consumers shared and ate this food in transit. As one English writer in 1884 put it, "the existence of the railway sandwich and its spread throughout the country has long been a source of terror to the people and of anxiety to the medical fraternity."[22] If the fin de siècle elite in most of the West considered fast food mediocre and unhygienic, in Japan, mass-produced fare thrived. Indeed, the tradition of the *ekiben* (box lunch for train travelers) endures, providing a variety of healthy and inexpensive snacks and meals for commuters, vacationers, and tourists.[23]

The interplay among local, national, and transnational forces enabled food to find its way onto on the urban table. In the first half of the twentieth century, extensive networks and surrounding rural territories fed large metropolises while migrants brought new foods and eating habits to urban centers. Consider the consumption of charcoal-grilled meat (*asado*) in the capitals of pastoral economies, a rural custom incorporated by urban workers in the cities of Texas, Northern Mexico, Argentina, Uruguay, Australia, and Brazil. Still, these processes were neither simple nor linear, generating and encountering countertrends and conflicts. While asado might have entered laborers' weekend menu, Chinese and Mexican foods were met with skepticism across the United States, only to become part of national cuisine years later. On the other hand, over the first half of the twentieth century, migrants found employment and better living prospects in cities. They simultaneously faced poverty and misery as wars and economic crises interrupted and disrupted food supplies. The next section focuses on how urban centers and dwellers navigated food scarcity.

3 Feeding Cities in Times of Scarcity

Over the past century, although industrial capitalism and agricultural revolutions reduced farming's high vulnerability to climatic fluctuations, the quantity and quality of the food available to urban residents continued to suffer because of wars, military sieges, maritime blockades, revolutions, economic crises, and environmental disasters. During the first half of the 1900s, the two world wars, social revolutions, and the economic crisis of 1929 severely disturbed urban

---

[22] Qtd. in Corby Kummer, "Delicacies of the Dinig Car," *The New York Times*, November 28, 2018.
[23] Patricial Wells, "Fast Food on the Fast Track," *The New York Times*, June 20, 1982.

provisions and reduced city dwellers' purchasing power to acquire basic foods. As markets collapsed amid chaos and destruction, municipal governments and military commandos stepped in to restore supplies while dwellers themselves devised strategies to acquire food and took to the streets demanding better prices. These multiple crises deepened social and food access inequalities between rich and poor, rural and urban populations. This section examines the public and social efforts administrations (military or civilian) developed in cities to cope with food shortages, including rationing and intervention in supply chains.

Battles for Food

Mexico City, 1915 – the so-called Year of Hunger – illustrates how civil and military conflicts disrupted inland food provision and residents' daily lives. In the early stages of the Mexican Revolution (1910–17), "consumer rebellions" sprang up all over the city; they demanded water, bread, and meat, which were disappearing from local groceries and butcher shops. These demonstrations spiked in 1915, when more than 5 percent of the capital city's population died (McCaa, 2003: 379–80). Earlier that year, Villista, Zapatista, and Constitucionalista forces had occupied Mexico City. Each party controlled the supply of essential items for residents' subsistence: Zapatistas regulated corn, flour, vegetables, sugar, and charcoal provisions while the other groups oversaw animal products traffic, petroleum and fuels trade, and foreign commerce. When these forces temporarily abandoned Mexico City, they cut off water and food supplies to inflict casualties on their enemies; grocers rationed the sale of corn, bread, and meat, among other items, even further. In the central, posh Roma neighborhood, a traveler witnessed "a multitude of more than 100 people shouting 'food, food, flour, corn … down with *gachupines* hoarders'"[24] (qtd. in Ramírez Plancarte, 2016: 382–400). Foodstuffs costs reflected such disruptions. According to the American Red Cross, between July 1914 and July 1915, corn prices in Mexico City increased by 2,400 percent; beans by 2,200; rice by 1,400; sugar by 940; and wheat flour by 900 percent. Pablo González, chief of the Constitutionalist forces that occupied Mexico City in the fall of 1915, judged such calculations excessive. By his account, corn costs had increased "only" about 1,300 percent; beans, 700; rice, 800; and flour, 400 percent. For reference, price fluctuations in Paris and London during World War I were moderate. In the first, six staple products increased their value by 153 percent

---

[24] The epithet was an overt reference to Spaniards, who had majorly run grocery businesses since colonial Mexico.

between July 1914 and July 1919; in London, during roughly the same period, the price of eight goods rose by 60 percent (Rodríguez Kuri, 2013: 156).

One explanation for such discrepancy is that whereas local administrative structures in Paris and London remained practically untouched, the Mexican Revolution (and the Russian Revolution later) destroyed these entities in Mexico's capital city – with dire consequences for citizens. Furthermore, success in food distribution rested on local, national, and international supply coordination. A comparative view of London, Paris, and Berlin shows that while the first two could mobilize resources in these supply layers, Berlin suffered because it lacked a centralized food production and distribution system. Paris established cooperatives for meat and grocery sales and created restaurants that served food at cost for munition workers. Informal practices also alleviated shortages: Parisians counted on countryside relatives to bring them food and extended family to stay in queues (Bonzon & Davis, 2007). They mitigated food scarcity by renting out spaces for gardening. In Paris and London, war gardens – in public spaces and private houses – provided urbanities with vegetables, potatoes, and eggs.

Significantly, public and military administrations' ability to coordinate food provision was boosted – or not – by their ability to convince dwellers that sacrifices were equitable. At the beginning of the war, Berliners accepted food substitutes (turnips, for instance) that barely resembled their prewar diet, rich in fats and proteins, but soon, the rationing system fueled the anger that erupted in rallies across the city. Additionally, Berlin's inconsistent regulations, requisitions, and edits undermined food distribution efforts. In 1915, millions of pigs were slaughtered to prevent food fit for human consumption from ending up as animal fodder. Such a move, however, strained processing and storage facilities. More importantly, excessive meat available in 1915 meant that Germans would go without it the following year. Indeed, in 1916, only half of the calories recommended by the War Office of Food were available. Soon, Germany's resources were stressed too thin. Across the country, chiefly in urban centers, around seven hundred thousand citizens perished from hunger (Weber, 2013).

The plight of Beirutis during World War I exemplifies how multiple factors, including poor relief coordination, inadequate transport infrastructure, and hoarding, combined with plagues and naval blockades, resulted in widespread famine. By late 1914, the Allies imposed a maritime blockade on the Ottoman Empire. Shortly after, Beirut's inhabitants hardly found wheat and flour. Municipal authorities appealed to grain merchants via Damascus and Aleppo, to no avail; when they found grains, they lacked transportation to bring cargo into the city. In February 1915, the local press declared that the city had only five days of stored grain. High prices followed suit, while available foodstuffs remained out of the poor's reach: for working-class Beirutis, high wheat and flour prices made their staple foodstuff – home-baked wheaten bread – unattainable, as competition for substitutes spiked. They temporarily compensated for wheat shortages by adding barley – a grain of the less affluent – to their bread flour, but as it climbed the social ladder, so did its prices. Natural disasters aggravated food shortages (Tanielian, 2012). In 1915, Palestine and Syria region suffered probably the worst recorded locust invasion. Clouds of insects darkened the skies in their path, leaving behind a devastated landscape. In Jerusalem, says Hasan al-Turjman, an Ottoman soldier stationed there, "flour and bread have basically disappeared ... Many people have not eaten bread for days." Later in the year, he continues, "I saw a throng of men, women, and boys fighting each other to buy flour near Damascus gate" (Tamārī & Turjman, 2011: 60, 89).

World War I also disrupted food provision away from the theater of war. Export hub cities like Buenos Aires and São Paulo or capitals like Lima and Santiago de Chile suffered because of large-scale shifts in maritime trade. In Buenos Aires, while public officials studied an agreement with the Royal Commission on Wheat Supplies to send Argentinean grains to the Allies, socialist legislators requested that the state distribute wheat and flour (initially destined for exports) to urban consumers across the country (Rapoport & Lazzari, 2014). Hoping to alleviate meat and bread shortages in its urban markets, Peruvian authorities prohibited wheat and flour exports. Such measures, however, did not prevent one of the most significant subsistence rebellions registered in early twentieth-century Lima. Although price increases ignited the revolts, the people saw the government's failure to supply its own cities as a "violation of traditional norms." In response, the urban poor in Lima ransacked public markets, stole railway food cargo, attacked groceries (mainly of Chinese property), and stormed wealthy neighborhoods, state offices, manufacturing works, and sugarcane farms (Ruiz Zevallos, 2001).

Similar riots and demonstrations occurred in other cities of the Americas. In 1919 Havana, 5,000 female workers from tobacco factories – despite being harassed by the police – marched and gathered in Parque de Trillo to protest high prices of rents and necessities (Garrido, 2020: 253–54). The same year, massive rallies took over the streets of Valparaiso, Antofagasta, and Santiago de Chile. A broad coalition of left-wing parties and organizations united behind the slogan "Consumption items are in the clouds!" They demanded fair prices for meat, milk, sugar, rice, coffee, butter, and charcoal (Rodríguez Terrazas, 2001). Meanwhile, the government set up and administered seven warehouses in Santiago's key areas, offering food at a cost. In August 1919, all butcher shops in the city closed their doors for three days. Dealing with low inventory – as most Argentinean cattle ended up in Europe to feed the British Army, thus depriving neighboring markets of herds – and hoarding by slaughterhouses, butchers hesitated to offer unaffordable meat to consumers, for "they did not want to appear as exploiters of people's misery" (qtd. in Rodríguez Terrazas, 2001: 124). Taking the law into their own hands, protesters looked for more, not less, state intervention to restore a "people's economy," hoping to get enough food (Ruiz Zevallos, 2001: 195). Subsistence demands that merged with labor rights struggles in 1918 Japan produced the iconic "rice riots." The summer revolts united rural and urban dwellers, together responding to the rising prices of staples caused by World War I. The unrest spread from villages to Kyoto, Osaka, Kobe, and Tokyo; per one account, ten million people participated in these uprisings, which represented a turning point in the country's history for their radical implications (Shōbei, 1966: 517; Yūko, 2022).

The agricultural disruptions the Soviets endured resulting from World War I and the 1917 Revolution were unparalleled. In 1920, as the English writer H. G. Wells put it, Russia had been "strained by six years of wars"; late that year, agricultural disasters in the Volga basin worsened matters (the area was one of the principal grain suppliers to Europeans). Yet, as Wells saw it, "the peasants look well fed" – a far cry from the assessment coming from those living in Saint Petersburg, which he describes as "a dismantled and ruined city" with collapsed services – communications, transportation, and drainage – abandoned shops and wrecked streets. Worse yet, the Soviet government could not procure enough food to feed locals; in addition, "collective control and rationing" delivered the "lowest grade ration."[25] And, indeed, their bread cards meant nothing when bakeries could not obtain flour. Sadly, deprivation in the autumn of 1920 presaged a more brutal winter. Volga's agricultural failures triggered a severe famine with global repercussions. By the summer of 1921, approximately thirty-seven million people were at risk of starvation in the country (Sasson, 2016a: 523). Hunger caused significant displacement, while Soviet government efforts to centralize the rural-urban food chain failed, sharpening the crisis.

A similar subsistence crisis provoked by droughts and floods befell China in the 1920s. Weak administrative coordination among local, regional, and national authorities made it impossible for the government to draw up a coherent relief program. It found itself subordinated to local and regional powers. The crisis spread from Manchuria to Shanghai, Pekin, and other industrial centers. Riots and rallies against scarcity and the cost of living ensued, threatening political order (Bergère, 1973).

---

[25] H. G. Wells, "Russia in the Shadow," *The New York Times*, November 7, 1920.

A decade after the Great War, the Great Depression exposed deep inequalities. Few illustrations convey the plight of urbanites during the 1930s economic crisis as people standing in bread lines and in front of soup kitchens in Chicago and New York City. Rural folk suffered as well; tenant farmers and sharecroppers lost their land to droughts and creditors, and with it, "livestock, poultry, [and] gardens to sustain them" (Poppendieck & Nestle, 2014: 30). But descriptions of scarcity and suffering dramatically contrasted with stories the US press was divulging about food dumping. Contemporaries called such events "the paradox of want amid the plenty" (Poppendieck & Nestle, 2014: xvi). While big farmers in Iowa and California disposed of corn and oranges, unemployed families in Philadelphia and Chicago scavenged for food. Furthermore, the end of World War I left many countries with overstocked goods; as wheat, corn, cotton, and coffee abounded in the international market, prices dropped, crashing primary export economies, including many in Latin America.

From its epicenter in the United States, the financial crisis shocked the capitalist economy, spreading its effects and upending the lives of millions around the globe. Urban centers worldwide saw the unemployed and working poor participate in massive hunger marches, as they did in Washington, DC, in March 1931. In British cities, more than two million unemployed men and women took to the streets demanding bread and beans and respect for their labor rights.[26] In Germany, the National Socialist government sought to boost its domestic arms and food industries, reducing imports of coffee, fodder for cattle, and other goods. The result was higher prices for butter and margarine (eaten by the poor), beef, pork, and bacon. In 1936, under Nazi rule, working-class Germans spent approximately half of their earnings on food; in Great Britain, they dedicated one-third of their income to those expenses. The crisis prompted cuts in food intake and disrupted other aspects of city dwellers' lives – like access to affordable housing.

In 1936 Geneva, the League of Nations (founded in 1919), prepared a report revealing that "large numbers of the working population even in the most advanced industrial countries are unnourished … [given their] inability to buy the right kinds of foods in the necessary quantities" (Eliot & Heseltine, 1937). In Great Britain, the urban working class might have had access to enough energy foods (sugar and flour) but lacked protective ones (milk and meat), while the wealthy feasted on meat, dairy products, fruits, and vegetables.

---

[26] "The 1930s Revisited: From Bread Lines to Hunger Marches: Street Photography in the 1930s," *The Guardian,* March 3, 2017; Juliet Gardiner, "The 1930s Revisited. Society: Are the 2010s Really Like the 1930s? The Truth about Life in the Great Depression," *The Guardian,* March 4, 2017.

Worldwide, the Great Depression strained governments at all levels, and pressured international and philanthropic organizations to develop policies to close this nutrition gap. Based on household food consumption surveys, the League of Nations codified standards for an average nutritious diet, establishing good eating and health benchmarks. Figure 5 shows an advertisement inspired by this type of study.

Latin American cities were impacted by and dealt with the Great Depression to varying degrees and in diverse ways. In Havana, the jobless and university students occupied public spaces condemning food shortages and high prices (Garrido, 2020). In Buenos Aires, at the behest of the General Labor Confederation and the Socialist Party, more than one hundred thousand people took to the streets demanding bread and work, occasionally looting grocery stores (Snitkofsky, 2013: 104). The widespread unrest was a blow to Argentina's military government, which initially resorted to repressive policies to deal with multiple crises. The Buenos Aires city council, for its part, created the Municipal Meat Packing Industry, expecting to manage supply, improve sanitary inspection, and control retail prices (Matocq, 1944). Readers of the local press wished that public officials would devote similar attention to open-air food markets – which sold fresh fish in deplorable conditions – and bakeries.[27]

Chile was one of the worst afflicted countries; global demand for nitrate – its primary export good – had already slowed in the 1920s. The crisis opened a decade of street confrontation between the left and the extreme right and political experiments like the Socialist Republic (June–September 1932). In Antofagasta, one of the country's exporting hubs, the collapse in nitrate and copper sales depressed economic activity and maritime traffic and shrank food imports (González Pizarro, 1999). Laid-off workers left mining camps and fled to provincial capital cities and Santiago, hoping to find jobs and assistance. Chilean authorities built on extant schemes to confront poverty and displacement, particularly in the country's capital, where more than a quarter of the country's population lived. In the city, the Ministry of Social Welfare, the Department of Labor, and charitable organizations built shelters, promoted unionization, sponsored recreational activities, and established public works. By the mid-decade, wage increase outpaced inflation; the poorest in Santiago could spend as much as 70 percent of their income on food. Bread, potatoes, and vegetables – the working-class staples – became unattainable, as did meat.

---

[27] "A través de la ciudad. Higiene y salubridad," *La Nación* (Buenos Aires), May 22, 1929, 8.

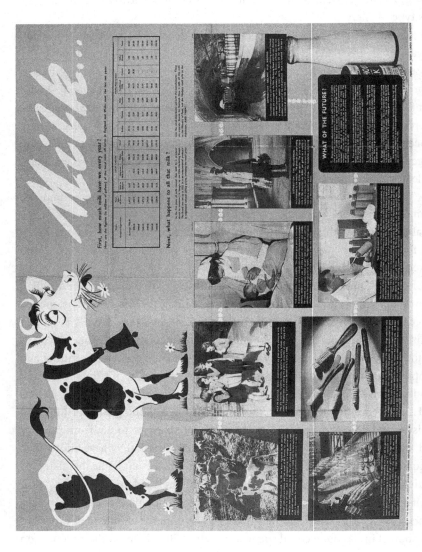

Figure 5 *Milk . . . The Role of Milk in Society after World War II.* Lithography by the Bureau of Current Affairs, 1946.

Dealing with Food Shortages

During the Spanish Civil War (1936–39), Barcelona and Madrid endured two long years under siege, circumstances that demanded first from municipal authorities and later from military commandos organized rationing schemes. In December 1936, Nationalist forces controlled more than half of Madrid – which housed around one million inhabitants – while the Republicans ran the "Red Military district," or one-third of the city. Inside the war zone, gardens and slaughterhouses barely functioned. In the long "Battle of Madrid" both sides weaponized food. Municipal authorities, people's commissions, and later the Madrid's Defense Board and its Supply Delegation devised a food-rationing system. Initially, medical doctors and nutritionists carefully planned standard food rations: milk, meat, bread, legumes, rice, coffee coal, condensed milk, soap, and cod fish to meet the needs of a complete diet with replacement parts (proteins), combustion (fats and sugar), water, salt, minerals, and vitamins (Tormo-Santamaría & Bernabeu Mestre, 2020). In April 1937, the legitimate Republican government established a National Food Security Institute, which promoted food literacy tailored to war times. It published pamphlets detailing foodstuffs' composition and nutrients and determining "adequate" rations. Books and manuals taught impoverished families to cook with meager ingredients and fuel. A consortium of municipal bakeries oversaw bread provision in early 1937. However, lack of provisions, black markets, and daily queues overwhelmed such plans (see Figure 6).

Madrileños' resistance was heroic; they had to forgo several foods as independent international organizations made milk available to convalescents and children (see Figure 7). Urban dwellers concocted war dishes: "evacuated stew" (onion, oil, water, and tomato pieces), "evacuated hake" (potato peels, dried cod waste, and oil), and bread soup (oil, water, and bread scraps). Without fuel, families burned furniture, clothes, and garbage for heating and cooking. Taking advantage of the acute bread shortage, Nationalists' airplanes dropped sacks of fresh wheaten bread in Madrid. When Republican Madrid was defeated, most residents lived on fewer than 830 calories daily (below starvation levels of 1,100 calories recorded during World War II), while thousands suffered from diseases related to vitamin deficiency (Gutiérrez Rueda & Gutiérrez Rueda, 2015: 66, 108–22).

The Battle of Madrid was a prelude to the misery, hunger, and destruction that befell the world a few years later. For military strategic reasons, everywhere in Europe during World War II, governments left rural populations to feed themselves and focused on the needs of urban and industrial centers. Malnourished workers did not deliver adequately in factories, hindering the arms industry;

Figure 6 No envieu els vostres productes al mercat lliure: Veneu-los a través dels Sindicats Agrícoles (Do Not Send Your Products to the Open Market; Sell Them Through Agricultural Unions), Evarist Mora Rosselló.

Source: Biblioteca de Catalunya, Original Publication, Direcció General d'Agricultura, [1937?].

equally relevant, continuous rationing and diminished food supplies could trigger internal unrest.

In Russia, the Soviet government devised a rationing program focusing primarily on cities, whereby the central state's stocks distributed food to their

Figure 7 Send Them Milk, Spanish Youthship Committee Appeal, 1939, Abram Games.

Source: ©Estate of Abram Games.

districts as early as 1940. The German invasion of the Soviet Union's breadbasket region (Belorussia, Ukraine, central Russia, and the Caucasus) disrupted its food production and transportation network, depriving the country of vital resources. Germany aimed to secure a territory to provide food for its nationals and to eliminate "useless eaters," including Slavs, Jews, and city dwellers.

Although messily implemented, the so-called Hunger Plan sought to disrupt supplies in urban settings and erode support for the Soviets (Berghoff, 2017; Garon, 2017). By 1944, laborers were indeed malnourished, and a sizable number died of starvation; still, the reaction against the state never materialized: "State food policy effectively organized scarce resources and had widespread popular support" (Goldman & Filtzer, 2021: 95). As the food needs of the Soviet Army increased, the state developed new rationing and relief schemes; although food allowances were well below dietary needs, urban settlements had at least minimum quantities of bread and sugar. Additionally, the state incentivized vegetable gardening and allowed peasants to trade their private plots' crops in the free market (Goldman & Filtzer, 2021).

Every aspect of Soviet civilian life was dramatically disrupted. Urban residents lacked all necessities, including housing, running water, fuel for heating and cooking, pans and other kitchenware, and clothing. Transportation practically halted; people walked to work through barricades, stepping over corpses and rats, whose population had exploded. In Moscow, "by the end of the winter [1942] every dog, cat and crow . . . had been caught and eaten" (Collingham, 2012: 327). Leningrad stands apart in World War II history; the city was under siege for nine hundred days (like Madrid years before) and lost almost one million lives, many of hunger (Goldman & Filtzer, 2021: 381). In the second half of 1941, daily bread rations for engineers, technicians, office and factory workers, adult dependents, and children dropped by more than one-half, with some improvement the following year. Citizens should have received other food allocations: meat, cereals, fish, macaroni, sugar, and fat, but very little of such provisions reached their tables; and only if they could withstand hours in queues – by 1942, more than six hours in January's freezing temperatures. In December 1941, Valerie Sukhov, a boy living in Leningrad, reminisced in his diary, "We cooked soup from carpenter's glue and ate all of the starch . . . Papa is prepared to eat the corpses of those killed in the bombardment. Mama refuses. It's already been a whole month since we had solid food in our stomachs, besides the daily portion of bread of 125 grams, there's been nothing" (Bidlack & Lomagin, 2012: 267–68).

In Great Britain, although resources were not equitably shared, and the poorer seldom enjoyed nonrationed foodstuffs, industrial hands could access more nutritious foods than before the conflict. The Ministry of Food established a canteen, or "British Restaurants," in every factory with more than 250 employees. In addition, waged workers could acquire a host of rationed food-stuffs, including meat, sugar, fats, and bacon, via a local retailer with whom they had registered. Their diets were monotonous, but they had uninterrupted access to bread and potatoes. In 1941, remittances from the United States via the Lend-Lease program, Commonwealth nations, and Argentina added much-needed fat and proteins to workers' tables. These circumstances are not meant to suggest that all people had enough or the food type necessary to keep fit. To be sure, food was unevenly distributed in households; for example, women and children ate less meat than men. Poor women were also responsible for rationing and queuing for food; hence, they could not tend and harvest their urban gardens like the British upper-middle class (Zweiniger-Bargielowska, 2017).

Middle East capitals, like Teheran, under Allied and British military control, also posed food and essentials supplying challenges to British diplomacy. The Anglo invasion of Iran in 1941 disrupted the country's domestic economy and foreign trade; between 1939 and 1943, food prices increased more than 500 percent. In December 1942, amid the Allied Middle East Supply Center's failure to adequately provision Tehran, university students – with diverse elitist interests – took to the streets demanding that the Iranian government provide higher bread rations and adopt counter-inflation measures. Public officials distributed food for the poor and imported American ovens to boost the bread industry. Still, the quantity and quality of such bread were unacceptable to Iranians' taste and necessities. Although the "Bread Riot" was more an elitist act of resistance (against occupation and food shortages) than a popular rebellion, the British command had to negotiate an Allied-Iranian economic convention. Soon after, Allied wheat arrived in Tehran to feed the city (McFarland, 1985).

Occupied France offers a case study of how poor and rich, urban and rural dwellers withstood World War II. Paris was a city of contrasts; while fancy restaurants served elaborate dishes, food kitchens scrambled to distribute basic foodstuffs. Residents could use ration cards to acquire subsidized items; bread was to be available daily, meat weekly, and sugar monthly. However, these items were scarce, and queuing became a way of life. To feed a three-member household, Parisians stood in line for approximately five hours every day. Company gardens, factory canteens, and cooperatives provided sustenance to undernourished industrial workers, as did low-priced restaurants and soup kitchens. Black markets became notorious in urban centers and, in some cases, were mechanisms for farmers to recuperate some of their expenses. In French cities, official rations were inadequate to satisfy adults' needs; in 1941, they amounted to approximately 1,500 calories per day (medical authorities recommended twice as much), dropped to approximate 1,250 in 1942, and below 1,000 in 1944 (Mouré, 2010: 268). Urban dwellers believed that farmers got richer amid their misery and that sacrifice was inequitable.

Urban inhabitants in Japan also begrudged their rural counterparts. Japan entered the war in late 1941; two years afterward, a full-blown American blockade cut off essential provisions from Korea, Manchuria, and Southeast Asia. In addition, American and British forces firebombed many food-producing areas. Japanese farmers fared better in part because they enjoyed food entitlements and benefited from policies that protected agricultural production. They provided food for the controlled market, saved items for hoarding, and delivered some goods to black markets but were forbidden to send provisions to city people.

Far from these theaters of war, Latin American municipal governments had to cope with two imperatives: boost industrial development and improve worker well-being. Concurrently, cities were overwhelmed by population growth, high inflation, increasing food costs, and shortages of essential goods, some of which were integral to the war effort, like fuels (coal, petroleum, gasoline, diesel), iron, industrial equipment, chemicals, medicines, and agricultural inputs (fertilizers, machines, agrochemicals). In Santiago and Valparaiso (Chile) and Buenos Aires, restrictions on diesel consumption disrupted rural-urban food chains, spiking household expenses. Yet, unlike cities on the war front, Latin American urban centers and their inhabitants coped with food shortages; they, in fact, experienced a recovery in quality of life in the 1940s.

One strategy that municipal governments employed to tackle supply and pricing disruptions was establishing public open-air food markets (*ferias libres*); the other was opening popular restaurants where workers could enjoy cheap and balanced meals. In 1939 Santiago, the city's first female mayor, the socialist Graciela Contreras, launched six ferias libres across poor and affluent neighborhoods. These were not merely top-down programs; labor unions and consumer activists mobilized in favor of these initiatives, as they did for state-sponsored restaurants (*restaurantes populares*) (Frens-String, 2021; Yáñez Andrade, 2019). Three years earlier, Santiago had opened its first restaurante popular in the upper-class Providencia barrio. At the inauguration ceremony, the regidor portrayed the eatery as an effort to "remediate . . . the suffering and misery of the proletarian class" and counter the "infiltration of unhealthy ideas that lead to desolation and social peace dismemberment" (Yáñez Andrade, 2016: 130). These broad associations between social peace and worker well-being were on display in early 1936 when Santiago hosted the Regional Labor Conference. At that juncture, the Peruvian delegation showcased their experiences with restaurantes populares implemented in its capital city and main port (Callao) earlier in the decade (Drinot, 2005). These eateries were meant to serve multiple purposes of urban social engineering: to offer nutritious, low-cost food to workers, to educate them on the benefits of such diet and hygiene, to promote a version of national cuisine, and, in some way, to strengthen control of urban classes. Soon after, Brazil launched its version of the restaurante popular.

In 1938, President Getúlio Vargas (1930–1945) established the "worker's basic food ration" and, two years later, the minimum wage. In August 1940, his government launched the *Serviço de Alimentação da Previdência Social* (Social Security Food Service), which managed cooperatives, selling staples at low cost and installed state-sponsored restaurants and workplace lunchrooms in Rio de Janeiro (then Brazil's capital city), Niterói, São Paulo, Fortaleza, Juiz de Fora, and Santos (Fogagnoli, 2011; Muniz, 2018). In Brazil, as in Chile and Peru, most food programs, including state-sponsored restaurants, were concentrated in urban areas. Although warranted, such a focus on urban dwellers also had other aims. In Lima, apart from serving the previously cited goals, restaurantes populares stood in dramatic contrast to Asian-run eateries that sold inexpensive, quick meals to the urban poor. State-sponsored restaurants presented an alternative to Asian eateries in the food they served (wholesome and purportedly national) and in the eating experience they offered (hygienic and ethical), shaping Limeño workers' identity along class and racial lines (Drinot, 2005; Yáñez Andrade, 2016). Other political and cultural subtexts were operating. In Peru, the leftist *Alianza Popular Revolucionaria Americana* (APRA, American Popular Revolutionary Alliance) administration first envisioned and implemented restaurantes populares. Right-wing governments adopted them when tensions ran high, and fresh social and labor movements threatened stability in Lima and across the country. These eateries established benchmarks for wholesome meals, for the conditions of an eating facility (clean, efficient, and organized), for the behavior of the "dignified" worker, and – most importantly, for measuring governments' commitment to the urban working class (Drinot, 2005).

Controlling foodstuff prices was another strategy municipal governments in Latin America utilized to manage disrupted supplies, which yielded ambiguous results. Buenos Aires and Mexico City accompanied such measures with ambitious plans to renew the urban food trade infrastructure, open central fruit markets, improve slaughterhouse sanitation, modernize drainage, and inspect food, especially of meat. But these measures only went so far; in New York City, representatives of neighborhood associations rallied on street corners distributing fliers from the Office of Price Administration (OPA) urging passersby to fight price gouging and black markets. In one of these demonstrations, women with baby carriages held signs reading, "Keep prices down, pay no more than the ceiling," and "The OPA can't do the job alone."[28] OPA's mandate to manage rationing and pricing during World War II simultaneously encouraged citizens to do their part for the war effort (saving lard, repurposing recipes, checking price lists) and strengthened consumer rights. State intervention and regulation had put

---

[28] "Queens Women Fight Food Black Market," *The New York Times*, April 13, 1945.

more animal proteins, for instance, on the tables of working-class families, but as the war dwindled, so did support for OPA. Trade associations and farmers' organizations claimed that price controls would break their industries and result in scarcity; meat producers went further, withholding cattle from the market. Consumers, for their part, fearing bare cupboards and more "meatless" days, sided with the industry (Jacobs, 1997). As the federal government pulled out of domestic food policies (envisioned in the Great Depression and strengthened during World War II) – it did not shy away from using food as an international political tool, particularly during the charged Cold War years, as the next section illustrates.[29]

4 A New Food Order Tackles Old Urban Dilemmas

After World War II, reconstruction and developmentalist projects swept the globe. Equitable food access was at the top of urban agenda in the Global South and Eastern capital cities, where authorities intervened in food markets, established price control of staples, and engaged in public campaigns against speculation. In Asian and African cities, such as Beirut, Alexandria, Cairo, Hanoi, Algiers, Calcutta, and Karachi, decolonization raised expectations that political independence would improve quality of life and expand access to consumable goods. Feeding cities during the Cold War remained the responsibility of local authorities and attracted the interests of international intergovernmental organizations, humanitarian agencies, and transnational businesses. Concurrently, urbanities forged new identities based on the right to buy safe and abundant goods (including foodstuffs) and enjoy free time. Transportation and housing projects allowed the wage laborers, albeit a small segment, to separate their personal from working lives and embrace the concept of privacy. These urban collective conventions and expectations were present in both capitalist and socialist cities. Although planned economies emphasized collective needs rather than individual demands, personal consumption was not absent in the eastern bloc. This section examines how the food governance that emerged after World War II materialized in cities, where consumer rights were most apparent and collective actions for safe and adequate food provisions reached global horizons.

Occupying Cities, Reshaping Diets

In late 1945, the *New York Times* radio broadcasted a debate titled "What Should America Do to Win the Peace in Europe?" The panelists claimed that the

---

[29] Charles Grutzner Jr., "Eating Places Seek Right to Serve Liver, Tong on Meatless Days," *The New York Times*, March 7, 1945.

Truman administration was unprepared for peace and warned that "American prosperity, as well as the peace of the world, depends on a healthy, well-fed Europe."[30] This call-to-action conference urged the United States to play a comprehensive role in postwar Europe and emphasized the global ramifications of feeding politics. It misrepresented one aspect of American food policies, however; as an agricultural superpower, between 1946 and 1947, the United States readily inundated the global market with wheat and flour in exchange for political allegiance. These shipments were credited with appeasing organized workers hungry for bread in France and tipping the balance in favor of the "free world" in Tehran, Cairo, Alexandria, Athens, and Istanbul. Although ascribing causality between food rations and political leanings is impossible, these deliveries foregrounded food diplomacy and set the stage for a new international food order.

Nowhere were such entanglements more visible than in postwar occupied cities. As urban experiences in German and Japan revealed, cities were ideal reconstruction postcards for their linkages with industrialization and political stability; feeding policies conditioned both. First, industrial productivity increase depended upon a well-fed labor force. In 1946, occupation officials in Japan assessed with great alarm that, since 1940, "labor output per [coal miner had] dropped from 14 tons per month to 5.3 tons, as the caloric intake dropped."[31] Second, in the war's aftermath, a stable food supply in cities could prevent social unrest, foster political support for occupying powers, and facilitate regime consolidation. Finally, cities were spaces for contested foodways. Emergency relief took ideological undertones in the early Cold War. The Berlin Airlift campaign – discussed ahead – reveals as much. Alongside these imperatives, other considerations were at play in the effort to "remake the conquered peoples," as a 1945 *New York Times* headline referred to Germans and Japanese.[32] US officials prioritized the former over the latter – few Americans had sympathy for Germans and even fewer for the Japanese. Milk rations for Japanese schoolchildren seemed more palatable when the occupation was at its initial stages. However, disappointed public health officers decried not having enough "complete" and "real" food for the urban population, or "bread and butter" (Bobrow-Strain, 2011: 88). The centrality officials ascribed to these items indicate how they envisioned food aid to Japan: fertilizers for rural folk

---

[30] "Well-Fed Europe Held Vital to Us," *The New York Times*, October 3, 1945.

[31] Foreign Office, File 371, Far Eastern. Japan. 69875, General Headquarters, Supreme Commander for the Allied Powers (1948). *Food Situation during the Second Year of Occupation*. Tokyo.

[32] "Shaping a New World: Remaking the Conquered Peoples: Japan and Germany under Occupation," *The New York Times*, September 23, 1945.

and better diets for urban dwellers. By contrast, occupying authorities in Germany did not concern themselves with "improving" the German diet but rather engaged in an agricultural revamping program.

The Berlin Airlift campaign (1948–49) epitomized the occupying powers' urgency to maintain a stable Berlin and underscored the city's significance in Cold War disputes. After World War II, Great Britain, France, the United States, and the Soviet Union controlled one city sector each, which they provided with necessities. In March 1948, the first three united, while Russia left the Allied Control Council and cut off traffic between Berlin and the West. American and British forces responded by airlifting food (including flour and Hershey's candies) and coal to Berlin over fifteen months.[33] While West Germans reframed the US and British powers – previous war enemies – as allies and the Soviet Union as their foe, the free world experienced a related transformation. In a press conference three years before the campaign, General Dwight Eisenhower justified the US decision to export foodstuffs to Germany, affirming to have "no intention of making the Germans fat [but to coordinate] ... minimum subsistence arrangements, [by which they] would receive only the bare amount of food necessary to stave off malnutrition and diseases ... about 2,000 calories daily."[34]

The need to rationalize US aid to Germany shifted after the partial Berlin blockade. Although the airlift campaign was a tremendous technical accomplishment – delivering more than 2.3 million tons of supplies to the city – it "failed to meet West Berlin's food needs, and the planes never even attempted to supply coal to heat private homes."[35] During the "Hunger Years" (1945–49), ration cardholders were not guaranteed enough food to keep them fit. Some goods were often unavailable, spoiled, or substituted for low-grade items. Food access was utterly unequal, resting on Berliners' social, political, and economic standing more than on the area in which they lived. Beyond that, the imagery of candy falling from the sky signified the abundance of the West (the United States, specifically) – "generosity, deliciousness, and satiety" in contrast with the Soviet Union, "a desolate space of tasteless food, widespread hunger, and arbitrary restrictions on consumers." These opposing images, "self-evident in the Western imagination ... were postwar inventions" (Weinreb, 2017: 117). These impressions lasted several decades, informed how the West (and beyond) saw the foodways of both worlds, and had a global reach. Consider this 1953 headline of a Bagdad newspaper: "East Germans Rush to West Berlin for Free

---

[33] Emily Towe, "Airlift Impresses Germans," *The Sunday Star Pictorial Magazine*, January 2, 1949.

[34] Gladwin Hill, "Must Feed Reich, Eisenhower Says," *The New York Times*, August 31, 1945.

[35] Paul Steege, "Cold War Myths," *The New York Times*, June 13, 2008.

Food Gifts"[36]; and a 1961 entry in the same daily about the Soviet Permanent Exposition, advertising "Electrical Appliances; Bicycles, Motorcycles and Scooters, Cameras, all kinds of Watches and Clocks, Household Sewing Machines and Foodstuffs."[37]

US officials in Japan went beyond these Cold War imperatives, envisioning emergency aid as a gateway to overhauling the island's agricultural makeup and its inhabitants' diets. Given the loss in food imports and domestic twin crises of poor weather and lack of workforce – the 1945 harvest was one of the worst in the century – Japan could not feed itself. In 1946, major cities' reliance on imported food fluctuated between 100 percent in Tokyo, around 80 percent in Osaka, Kanagawa, and Aomori, and over 50 percent in Hyogo (Aldous, 2013: 60). In several Japanese cities, residents' food expenses accounted for 70 percent of their budget; sources often described urban dwellers as "undernourished." In Tokyo, attendants of the 1946 May Day Parade carried banners and chanted slogans demanding political renewal and workers' rights; above all, they asked for food; one sign read "Give us Enough Food."[38] Two years on, the situation remained dire; a report prepared by the Supreme Commander for the Allied powers related that urban residents in Japan were "at risk of 'acute malnutrition' or starvation," for they depended almost entirely on imports of wheat, flour, and maize.[39] These alarming statements subtly conveyed that the Japanese diet was imperfect, while food policies revealed pervasive preconceived notions about what constituted good eating. To build better bodies occupation officials believed, the Japanese diet needed more animal proteins and carbohydrates (Aldous, 2013).

Not far from Japanese cities, the Chinese Communist Revolution (1945–49) abruptly changed China's social-agricultural makeup through collectivization. In the winter of 1961, after stiff resistance and strikes in Hunan, the Chinese Communist Party imported grains from Western countries and developed rationing systems in Beijing, Tianjin, Shanghai, and Liaoning, hoping to alleviate social tensions. Revolutionary cadres also organized free communal halls and kitchens that fed more than 64 percent of the rural population (Graziosi, 2017: 66, 77). Shanghai, a city that had survived the Japanese occupation during World War II and had once been "China's gateway to Modernity," descended into chaos (Bergère, 2017), facing rural exodus, overcrowding, economic

---

[36] *The Iraq Times* (Bagdad), July 30, 1953.
[37] "The Soviet Permanent Exhibition in Bagdad," *The Iraq Times* (Bagdad), June 11, 1961, 8.
[38] Burton Crane, "Japanese Parades Stress Food Needs," *The New York Times*, May 2, 1946.
[39] Foreign Office, File 371, Far Eastern. Japan. 69875, General Headquarters, Supreme Commander for the Allied Powers (1948). *Food Situation during the Second Year of Occupation*. Tokyo.

collapse, unemployment, and hunger. In these politically charged times, however, some in the "Nationalist Products Movement" pushed for a boycott of US grains and flour (Yao, 2017: 1440, n. 4).

Food Geopolitics in the Kitchen and the City

The contrast between abundance and scarcity shaped new theories about revolutions, global capitalism, development, and urban life. Far from reconstruction zones, cities in the Americas experienced sustained industrial development; their citizens benefited from employment expansion and wage increases. With income growth, the rising urban poor and middle classes relied on their incomes to access goods and services and to improve their overall well-being. In Latin America, between 1945 and 1955, purchasing power and living standards rose (particularly in the most industrialized urban economies), although high price increases deepened inequalities and weighed heavily on the poorest. Governments adopted anti-inflationary policies and beefed up or created safety net programs, including pension and health benefits, child protection services, and food price controls. State-run companies and new government agencies distributed basic foodstuffs at low prices and introduced consumer-protection policies, which benefited the working and middle classes.

In the developmentalist era, urbanization and industrialization pushed local authorities to overhaul food provision infrastructures. In the 1950s and 1960s, Rio de Janeiro and Mexico City underwent significant urban renewal. Rio's mayor, Ângelo Mendes de Morais (1947–51), advertised his achievements with great fanfare in a newspaper article entitled "Federal District's Food Increasingly Comes from Itself." Morais's administration remodeled the municipal slaughterhouse, expanded the open-air markets (*feiras livres*) network, incentivized horticulture, built food depots, granted loans for poultry and egg producers, and refurbished milk plants.[40] In Mexico City, Regent Ernesto P. Uruchurtu (1952–66) opened several food markets, seeking to streamline food supply chains to feed a capital in constant growth. He inaugurated La Merced central market, with thousands of stalls, and established "popular markets" in neighborhoods where small producers from nearby areas sold fresh goods at affordable (even subsidized) prices. Uruchurtu also led the building of a massive public slaughterhouse; Ferrería (as it was known) represented the technological apex of meat industrialization in the city. These transformations, however, temporarily disturbed wholesale and retail channels, especially in the cases of meat and milk, causing shortages (Arellano Ramírez, 2020).

---

[40] Newton B. Melo, "A comida do distrito federal vem cada vez mais dele mesmo," *Diário Carioca*, January 20, 1950.

To manage food supply disruptions, the Mexican government also created various state food agencies, like the 1960s *Compañía Nacional de las Subsistencias Populares* (CONASUPO, National Popular Subsistence Company), a parastatal organization whose mission was to regulate the trade of staples and protect low-income consumers. It intervened in the marketing of barley, beans, copra, corn, cotton, rice, sesame, sorghum, soybeans, sunflower, and wheat, supporting local producers' prices and handling imports. CONASUPO officials sought to control the entire supply chain; production and distribution improvements were essential to providing adequate food for the expanding urban poor and low-middle-class (Ochoa, 2000). In New Delhi and other decolonized Indian cities, similar goals were behind the Food Corporation of India, launched in 1964, almost two decades after independence from British rule and Partition. This public-private partnership corporation engaged in price support and market regulation to protect farmers, aiming to allocate adequate food for India's growing population; it also managed grain imports primarily from the United States.[41]

Back in the Americas, in Lima, members of APRA crafted a master plan for the city that entailed price regulation; reconstruction and reorganization of butcher shops, meatpacking, and street commerce; and food provision inspections.[42] Latin American cities and other capitals in the Global South were laboratories of development and new state-oriented food policies against social unrest and inequalities that created homogeneous consumption habits. The Buenos Aires of 1952 offers a snapshot of how expenditure on public services and welfare, employment, and standard of living improvement enabled the masses to participate in cultural experiences, including dining out. That year, approximately five million urbanities monthly visited cinema halls, theaters, sporting events, and the city's zoo, eating at restaurants while they enjoyed these experiences (Milanesio, 2014: 124). Attuned to the new consumer buying power and the ravages inflation could cause, Juan Domingo Peron's government (1946–55) waged "wars" against speculation and in favor of "loyal retailing." These advertising and political awareness campaigns targeted urban women, no longer portrayed as household guardians but as active consumers (Elena, 2007: 129). Postwar-conscious females challenged stereotypes of homemakers and mothers; in their daily visits to Buenos Aires (see Figure 8) commercial districts and food markets, they found new goods and expected them to be safe to consume.

---

[41] "India to Build Up 5,000 000-Ton Buffer Food Stocks," *The Iraq Times* (Bagdad), February 2, 1960, 5.

[42] "La Junta Municipal transitoria de Lima afronta el problema alimentario," *Urbanismo: Órgano del Buró Nacional Aprista de Municipalidades*, 1, Num. 1 (Lima), August 1946.

Figure 8 Buenos Aires, gente en la calle Florida con anuncio de Café Paulista de Brasil, circa 1950 (Buenos Aires, People on Florida Street with an Advertisement for Café Paulista from Brazil).

Source: Colección Nacho López, Fototeca Nacional, Instituto Nacional de Antropología e Historia, Mexico City.

Urban authorities in socialist cities of central Europe also engaged in public campaigns against food price speculation and black markets after World War II. In Warsaw, those campaigns focused on women as buyers and workers in grocery stores (Mazurek & Clavier, 2013). Industrialization and the expansion of the female workforce went hand in hand with hopes of overhauling the food industry and urban tastes. In Russia, while these innovations freed women from the conventional homemaker's role, the state also incentivized motherhood. Mass-produced foods abounded and saved women time; concurrently, however, they were tasked with preserving traditional food and domesticity (Jacobs, 2019). Such incongruity also operated in market economies that portrayed women at once as rational homemakers, conscious consumers, and vessels of tradition. In the food realm, planned and market economies had much in common, except for the former's emphasis on socialized dining; both promoted scientific diets, abundance, and consumer experience. Inspired by industrial farming in the United States, Nikita Khrushchev's (1953–64) corn crusade sought to increase the seed's yield for livestock fodder and expand urban consumption of meat (pork, beef) and milk. Although it did not deliver a socialist life of plenty, Khrushchev's reforms set the stage for a consumer-centered approach during the Brezhnev era (1964–82) (Hale-Dorrell, 2015).

Collaboration and competition between the United States and the Soviet Union played out on several fronts. The "Kitchen Debate" in 1959 – a series of impromptu conversations between Khrushchev, the Soviet Premier, and Vice President Richard Nixon during the American National Exhibition in Moscow, one of which occurred in the American kitchen booth – provided images of American prowess in farming, ingenuity, and abundance. Khrushchev also envisioned showcasing Russia's industrial ingenuity via mass-produced foods – frozen vegetables, preserved fruits and jams, and items unfamiliar to the Soviet consumer such as "instant mashed potatoes and frozen french fries" (Hale-Dorrell, 2015: 182), accessible to all. However, as in the case of agricultural overhaul, factory production fell short of the quota. Even public dining halls in major Soviet cities did not meet diners' demand. In the late 1950s, Leningrad offered "55.2 seats in cafeterias and dining-halls for every 1,000 citizens. Moscow followed just behind at 50.7 places" (Hale-Dorrell, 2015: 185).

Seeking a departure from the Stalin scarcity years, 1960s stability was to provide more than staples; state planners called for an increase in potato chips and popcorn sales in stands near subway stations in major Soviet urban centers. In the 1930s, one such treat was ice cream processed and distributed by state-run companies. The "socialist consumerism" of the 1970s went further, as the state actively procured special goods for the citizenry and bet on a state-socialist consumer culture. In the German Democratic Republic (GDR), urban dwellers enjoying subsidized housing, public transportation, and foodstuffs possessed disposable income to buy local and luxury items offered by government-owned-Delikat Stores, including specialty coffee. In Russia, Brezhnev's economic reforms expanded access to consumer goods and improved food safety, quality, and appearance, like his counterparts in the West. Consumers also demanded better and more choices, from tasty milk to fashionable clothing (Morard III, 2023). In 1970s Moscow, hundreds of retail stores included cafés, restaurants, and self-service dining halls, presenting shopping as an experience that went hand in hand with leisure (Chernyshova, 2013).

The New Consumer

Public awareness and suspicion – ripe with nationalistic undertones – about the quality of foodstuffs shone a new light on the food and drink industries and government programs worldwide. Although consumers in Tokyo and Paris came to access a more diversified food basket, they preferred "their" rice and apples over imported ones.[43] In Cairo and other major Egyptian cities, residents harshly decried the quality, flavor, and size of subsidized wheat bread or "national loaf" (Schewe, 2017: 54). Available since the 1950s, the national loaf was essential to policies implemented by President Gamal Abdel Nasser (1956–70). However, not all bread is created equal. Residents of Cairo (and Marrakech) defined "good bread" based on multiple sociocultural criteria, including cereal's provenance and quality and the loaf's taste, texture, and price (Graf, 2018: 228). Consumers vigorously disparaged fixed prices, black markets along bread's production chain, and government inspectors for their lukewarm response to corruption.[44]

Food was a contested terrain in international struggles – part of the broad 1960s and 1970s counterculture movement – that domestically converged with other demands and had different protagonists. Despite US food abundance – a weapon it had globally wielded since the early Cold War years – in Greensboro and Raleigh (North Carolina), San Antonio and Houston (Texas), and many cities of Southern states, lunch counter sit-ins "exposed how racial segregation impacted the ways in which blacks accessed food in public eating places" (Smith, 2020: 382). As Cold War tensions ran high, urban consumers inside and outside the United States criticized American institutions, targeting industrial white bread as a symbol of its economic power, geopolitical ambitions, and racial injustices (Brobow-Strain, 2011).

In the socialist world, young consumers in Leningrad and Moscow overtly challenged "Soviet Club" (*Komsomol,* state-sponsored clubs for the youth) gathering in "Youth Cafes" (*Molodezhnye Kafe*), where they savored coffee and meals, engaged in private conversations, and listened to jazz. From 1958 to 1964, these cafés offered vibrant socializing spaces (Tsipursky, 2016). New consumer-oriented policies arose in socialist Eastern Europe. The GDR's planned economy devised an ambitious program to cope with periodic food

---

[43] "Les Français préfèrent les pommes et dédaignent les abricots," *Combat: De la Résistance a la Révolution,* May 4, 1948, 1, 5.

[44] Michael Slackman, "Bread, the (Subsidized) Stuff of Life in Egypt," *The New York Times,* January 16, 2008.

shortages and provide German tables with coffee, oranges, and bananas; these goods were also central to citizens' diets in the Federal Republic of Germany. In July 1977, the Politburo developed new guidelines for coffee retailing in restaurants and prohibited its sale in factory canteens (Pence, 2012: 216). As Party officials disseminated information about a global coffee crisis, consumer outrage forced a reduction in prices; later, the state apparatus exchanged industrial goods (including military supplies) with foodstuffs from Cuba and African countries. GDR urban buyers channeled their consumer grievances by writing petitions noting that Cuban oranges were not orange-colored and its grapefruits too sour, and that "Kaffee Kosta" (packed and distributed by state-run companies) was of bad quality. Kaffee-Mix, the alternative beverage GDR bureaucrats promoted for working-class consumption, was anything but coffee (Dietrich, 2020).

Consumer anxieties and demands were contested urban issues beyond West/East spheres of influence (Ramsingh, 2011). Starting in the 1960s, a coalition of decolonized countries met in Havana and proposed a new international order and "just and equitable arrangements" to promote development, environmental protection, and food sufficiency (Prakash & Adelman, 2023). At the United Nations (UN) Conference in Nairobi (1976), leaders of the Non-Aligned Movement called for food safety rules to balance out the interests of exporters with the rights and health expectations of consumers in poor countries. In Rome, 1974, at the First World Food Conference, the UN translated these ideals into the Universal Declaration on the Eradication of Hunger and Malnutrition. An example of such efforts was the well-coordinated transnational campaign urban middle-class consumers led against powdered milk companies like Nestlé (e.g., the documentary *Bottled Babies*, 1976). Protesters focused on the dangers that market-driven economics and monopolies by food corporations posed to impoverished Third World mothers (Sasson, 2016b).

Consumer culture proved central to political struggles in Santiago de Chile, as women grew tired of austerity and marched through streets with empty pots during the latter years of the socialist government of Salvador Allende (1970–73). When tensions ran high, an anti-Allende publication praised supermarkets for embodying choice and freedom, a place where "everyone can buy . . . and everyone waits in the same line to pay, without special privileges" (Frens-String, 2021: 185–86). The erosion of consumer confidence was a powerful force against socialist regimes (Masterovoy, 2017). In East Germany, consumers craved coffee; because the regime lacked exchange to buy imports, the government added coffee to the list of staples and established relations with Brazil, Ghana, and Guinea. When the Berlin Wall came down, East Berliners rushed to the West's shops to acquire goods and foodstuffs they longed for, including bananas, which in the West symbolized recovery after World War II. Other tropical fruits and luxury items remained high on the list of these new consumers, who initially sought "Western" goods; when this enthusiasm faded, GDR's foods and recipes experienced a revival (Weinreb, 2017). A few years later, in Kella (a village on the Eastern Germany border), the smells and sounds associated with small animal rearing and vegetable growing also died out, for the town's residents acquired most produce, eggs, and meat in supermarkets (Berdahl, 1999). The next section examines how this innovation radically transformed food chains and urbanites' food experience to this day.

5 The Taste of Capitalism: Supermarkets, Convenience Foods, and Pervasive Inequalities

In the early twentieth century, Los Angeles introduced a revolutionary innovation in food marketing: the supermarket. This new convenience quickly spread – first to eastern cities (New York, Philadelphia, and Boston), and later, during the Great Depression, across the United States. Los Angeles's rich agro-industrial hinterland (for growing fresh produce) and highway system (fueled by petroleum, asphalt, and cars) enabled supermarkets to cater to a racially and economically segregated consumer population. Supermarkets transformed both ends of the food chain and institutional and socioeconomic environments. They also altered rural-urban network morphologies, challenged consumption habits, modified the entire nondurable goods chain, restructured agrifood industries, and rearranged traditional food retailing, including public markets. Across continents and political regimes, supermarket implementation adapted to specific urban conditions, evolving alongside food supply chain innovations and consumer cultures, functioning as a nexus of new technologies and urban markets, homogenizing foodstuffs and eating habits. This section studies the rise and dissemination of supermarkets; the globalization of convenience foods; and the urban inequalities in food access.

The Engine of Modernity (and Dietary Transition): the Supermarket

Supermarkets were not a novelty in mid twentieth-century Latin America. As Figure 9 shows, in December 1955, São Paulo – soon to become Brazil's most populous city – launched the third branch of *SirvaSe* or "Help Yourself" supermarket. It was part of the International Basic Economy Corporation (IBEC), a business Nelson Rockefeller created to "promote the economic development of various parts of the world" through agriculture and services

Figure 9 Supermercado SirvaSe.

Source: *Correio Paulistano*, December 20, 1955, São Paulo.

improvement (Durr, 2006: 13). In the 1950s, IBEC entered the retailing industry by implementing US-style supermarkets in Maracaibo and Caracas, Buenos Aires, Lima, and Milan. SirvaSe, as its name implies, broke the counter barrier between grocer and customer. The ad features a well-dressed woman pushing a shopping cart filled with goods she presumably purchased at SirvaSe. "At the new SirvaSe [proclaims the ad], you will find fresh food, rigorously selected, for the lowest prices! And with great ease: you choose what you want without waiting." Published days before Christmas, the ad also declares that the new SirvaSe is a "gift to the housewives of São Paulo." But it was, in fact, a gift to a few wealthy Paulistas who lived in affluent neighborhoods and owned a car, "if you live far away, [reads the line at the page's end] walk a little further . . . and serve yourself better." For those in São Paulo's peripheries, this proposition was not feasible.

No contemporary commercial supermarket (*hipermercado* in Portuguese) in São Paulo expects to entice customers to "walk" to their stores. Today, they are spread across the city – serving poor and rich neighborhoods – and a larger share of the population are car owners who drive to buy essential food items (fresh, frozen, and cooked foods, fruits, and vegetables), everyday necessities (personal hygiene products, medicines, clothing, and footwear), and even furniture, electronics, appliances, and hardware; the list is long. Between the 1950s SirvaSe and the 1980s hipermercado, enormous technological and socioeconomic developments took place in Brazil and elsewhere. At the local and regional levels, governments invested in reliable transportation, electricity, and water infrastructure (roads, sanitation, and inspection stations) that connected big farms to supermarkets and provided urban centers with essential services. At the transnational level, megacorporations bought meat and dairy products and featured fresh produce (similar in shape and color) in supermarket display cases. For their part, transnational trade and sanitary agreements enhanced goods exchanges and seasonless eating. Finally, at the household level, aside from a car, shoppers might have acquired appliances (blender, mixer, refrigerator, freezer, or microwave) to store and cook the items they purchased, presumably at the same store where they bought the family's food. These changes speak to late twentieth-century globalization and, most notably, to the revolution in distribution and management that linked agribusiness to supermarkets. Such innovations were meant to lower food prices for urban populations, wipe out small retailers, and change consumption patterns unfolded differently everywhere (Hamilton, 2018).

In its ideal formulation, supermarkets aimed to create an urban marketplace of plenty and low-priced foods. Such a scheme did not materialize quickly in cities outside the United States, however. For instance, in Caracas, the IBEC venture sought to industrialize agricultural and distribution systems in Venezuela, but initially, it failed on both grounds. First, US Midwest farming methods could not be transplanted to tropical environments. Second, development in infrastructure and distribution was only in its infancy in Venezuela, making goods transportation costly (Hamilton, 2018). As a result, the company turned to retail, relying on US imports rather than local foods and catering to upscale customers.

Where supermarkets entered, traditional retailing also proved highly resilient. In Milan, small grocers, local retailers, myriad vendors, and politicians overtly opposed Supermarkets Italiani, a 1957 IBEC venture. In 1966 Buenos Aires, small business organizations distributed fliers denouncing supermarkets, which they labeled "privileged ... and dominated by monopolies."[45] Three years later, urban guerrillas in Argentina went further. During the Cold War, anti-imperialists in the Global South cast supermarkets as a symbol of international exploitation and US consumerism. Against this politically charged background, guerrilla organizations targeted MINIMAX (minimum prices, maximum quality) supermarkets – another IBEC/local partnership. Ahead of a visit by New York governor Nelson Rockefeller to Argentina, Buenos Aires residents woke up on June 26, 1969, to learn that thirteen branches of MINIMAX stores had been scorched in the early morning; eight of them reported a total loss.[46] Three years earlier, a Rockefeller supermarket in Caracas suffered a similar attack.[47]

Despite disrupting food supply chains and local retailers, supermarkets did not always wipe out competitors. Founded in 1955, the Buenos Aires SUPERCOOP (*Cooperativa El Hogar Obrero*) retained control, from production to retail, of dairies, poultry and red meat, fresh goods, flour, and bread, and managed 290 supermarkets across Argentina's leadings cities for the next two decades. Most notably, supermarkets clashed with city governments' food provision mandates. Amid Mexico's rapid economic growth and industrialization, its capital city population practically doubled between 1940 and 1960. To handle high inflation, on several occasions, the city and federal governments created state food agencies *Compañía Exportadora e Importadora Mexicana, S. A.* (Mexican Export and Import Company) (1949) and CONASUPO, aiming at establishing direct channels between farmers and consumers and providing subsidized goods for the population, with a focus on city dwellers. CONASUPO managed shops countrywide; in 1970, rural stores accounted for only a fraction of urban ones (Zazueta, 2011). Concurrently, Mexico's private interests bet on supermarkets. In the 1950s, a Northern Mexican business group sought to tap

---

[45] *Propósitos* (Buenos Aires), 5ta época, Año XVI, March 27, 1969.
[46] "Buenos Aires, terrorismo y disturbios: El lenguaje de la furia." *Revista Siete Días Ilustrados* (Buenos Aires), June 30, 1969.
[47] "Rockefeller Store in Caracas Is Raided," *The New York Times*, September 14, 1963.

into the country's largest urban market and introduced Super Mercados S.A. or SUMESA, a private supermarket chain, to Mexico City; a Spanish Mexican business group founded COMERCIAL MEXICANA, and another, GIGANTE supermarkets. Nevertheless, much like the Brazilian SirvaSe, in their first years, SUMESA, GIGANTE, and COMERCIAL MEXICANA served only clientele in the cities' affluent districts (Bleynat, 2021; Cerutti & Rivas Sada, 2006).

Consumers on the outskirts – the majority – continued to rely on public and open-air markets, and local grocers because of proximity, convenience, credit, and prices. In large cities, particularly after 1980, retail store locations reveal inequalities in consumers' purchasing power, undermining investors' claims that big chains would improve food access for the urban poor. In Cape Town, supermarkets privileged patrons in wealthy districts. Although they also clustered in high-traffic areas near highways and mass transit hubs, informal food retailers remained essential in underserved neighborhoods (Battersby & Peyton, 2014). Today, urban shoppers in sub-Saharan Africa who cannot afford to buy in bulk at supermarkets make frequent purchases with neighborhood informal vendors (Davies *et al.*, 2021). In the early 2000s Hanoi, when the introduction of supermarkets was in its early stages in Vietnam, poor shoppers visited different outlets. According to one customer, "The supermarket? No! We never go. We're too poor! ... With my salary, I can't afford to shop at the supermarket. I know that vegetables are safe and guaranteed, but they cost twice as much as outside (on the markets) ... If supermarket prices go down, then everyone can buy there" (Figuié & Moustier, 2009: 213).

The global expansion of commercial supermarkets worldwide took distinct paths, and consumers' shopping behavior followed diverse patterns. In 1990s São Paulo, despite having access to different types of supermarket formats, Paulistas continued to visit their neighborhood feiras. They bought staples and nonperishable items at commercial chains once a month and farm-sourced items at feiras weekly. In 1999, approximately 1,000 open air markets sold 70 percent of fresh food in the city. Shoppers explained their preference for feiras because of quality: "The stall owned by Serafim is the best stall in the feira [says one customer]. He is already famous ... and his products seem to be always the most beautiful" and because of vendors' trustworthiness (Zinkhan, Fontenelle & Balazs, 1999: 14). Feiras livres offer a space for social exchange, bargaining, and personal relationships. As another shopper stated, "Sometimes I even cash a check with Da. Conceição [stall owner] ... When I don't have any money and don't have time to go to the bank, she cashes it for me ... Everything [is] based on friendship" (Zinkhan, Fontenelle & Balazs, 1999: 14). As these examples show, commercial chains did not eliminate traditional retailing; instead, they complemented and influenced each other. For instance, to boost fresh vegetable and fruit sales, Carrefour (a French *supermarché* established in São Paulo in 1975) instituted feiras every day (*feiras todos os dias*). In South African cities, while supermarkets might have forced greengrocers and corner stores to close their doors, peddlers in low-income areas carried on with their business (Crush & Frayne, 2011).

The supermarket model – based on centralization, distribution efficiency, cleanness, and abundance – appealed to capitalist and socialist consumers and politicians alike. Urban food customers in Hungary, Yugoslavia, and the GDR thrived on self-service retailing that resembled, in many respects, US supermarkets. After a period of scarcity and rationing, from 1945 to 1970, these countries sustained agricultural, transport, and commercial development, making them ripe for a supermarket of sorts, shelves packed, and consumer experience. Socialist supermarkets offered plenty of convenience goods that saved time for all – but working women, in particular. They lacked fresh produce and fruits, as revealed by the comments of attendees at the 1957 Zagreb International Trade Fair. Housewives who poured into the halls of the US exhibition marveled at packed, price-marked, and clean meat, grapes, "crisp green vegetables," "beautiful corn," and "tasty bananas."[48] After the Zagreb fair, a state-owned corporation installed more than twenty supermarkets across Yugoslavia, the majority in Belgrade (Hamilton, 2018). Years later, these stores stocked up with frozen foods and ready-to-make meals.

Other aspects distanced socialist supermarkets from their Western counterparts. First, in the United States, despite heavy state investment in agricultural technology and goods distribution, supermarkets were upheld as the pinnacle of free enterprise. In planned economies, given that the state was the ultimate food purveyor, they served to showcase their agricultural system prowess. It worked better in Yugoslavia (albeit temporarily) and Eastern Germany than in Russia, where Khrushchev's agricultural revolution did not deliver the immediate expected results. After the Brezhnev era's reforms, by the mid-1970s, major Soviet cities counted with US-style supermarkets. Second, in urban Eastern Europe, self-service groceries were at walking distance from shoppers' houses, a departure from the US supermarkets and their Latin American iterations that catered to the motorized consumer (Patterson, 2009). Third, urban dwellers in socialist cities accessed food variously: corner stores, groceries, supermarkets, and state-run cooperatives. These stores stood alongside a structured system of collective eating, school cafeterias, and workplace canteens. The latter

---

[48] Elie Abel, "Typical American Supermarket Is the Hit of Fair in Yugoslavia," *The New York Times*, September 8, 1957.

continued to play an essential role in the lives of working Germans after reunification, who considered the closure of canteens an erosion of their East German identities (Thelen, 2006).

From the early 1900s, another type of supermarket evolution occurred in urban centers where the Chinese migrant community was highly represented. In Lima, Chinese-owned grocery stores like the Wong family business developed into commercial supermarkets across the city (Lock Reyna, 2006). In London, Birmingham, and Manchester, since the 1960s, Hong Kong migrants formed a so-called Chinese food chain: large family-based companies that imported packaged and frozen foods from Hong Kong to wholesalers, supermarkets, small retailers, restaurants, and takeaway shops. They all contributed to expanding Asian food (Chinese, Indian, and Indonesian) consumption, especially street food (Cheung & Gomez, 2012). Across the urban United States (and Europe), the spread of bodegas accompanied the demographic Latin American migration shift; like their Chinese counterparts, some of these businesses evolved into supermarket chains.[49] In this sense, although US supermarkets and their iterations might differ in their origins, once established, both played a comparable role in disseminating convenience foods and homogenizing tastes.

Big food retail influenced small merchants, for instance, to stack their stores' shelves with cheap, processed food widely available in commercial chains, a decision that has had detrimental dietary ramifications. In 2000, urban communities in Guatemala that had more supermarkets ate less corn and beans and more processed foods than their rural counterparts (Asfaw, 2008). In four Zambian cities (Lusaka, Kitwe, Mansa, and Kasama), wheat became the dominant staple for middle- and high-income supermarket shoppers, while the poorest patronized informal retailers to buy maize (Crush & Frayne, 2011). On the other hand, supermarkets offer customers more food variety, including frozen fruits and vegetables (Hawkes, 2008: 266–67; Liao *et al.*, 2016).

Savoring New Foods

Aside from bridging countryside and city, supermarkets were the central locus of new convenience food distribution. Canning and freezing were old technologies, but fast-freezing innovation in the early twentieth century and packaging in plastic containers and wrappers later, better preserved food's appearance and taste and expanded the shelf-life of foodstuffs, converted into examples of ingenuity and efficiency. An article published in 1961 predicted that "more than one-third of the families in Western Europe will be eating frozen food

---

[49] Tina Vasquez, "A Nimble New York Grocery Store Follows Latino Immigration to the South," *The Guardian*, March 29, 2024.

regularly" by the mid-decade. Then, Birds Eye Foods, one of the largest US companies, controlled 70 percent of the British market, selling hamburgers and frozen dinners to Briton's taste, "fish and chips, beef and Yorkshire pudding, kidney and mushroom pies, fish fingers ... and kippers." On the Continent, frozen poultry and chicken rotisseries were ubiquitous; in Western Germany's streets, continues the article, "one can buy a half or a quarter of a chicken." France and Italy reportedly were "producing frozen gourmet meals" and pizza.[50] While such predictions might have reflected processors' optimism, frozen food retailing grew significantly in the past century, particularly in high-level urbanization areas worldwide.

Domestic refrigerator expansion, and microwaves, later, where households had access to the electric grid – accompanied the variety of frozen products marketed, from fruits, vegetables, and prepacked meats to baked goods and ready-to-eat meals.[51] These kitchen appliances remained financially out of reach for the decolonized poor urban population across Third World capital cities; until the 1990s "only 10 percent of black South Africans in urban areas had access to domestic electricity" (Lee, 2006: 55).

New industrial technologies revolutionized ancient staples and created new ones. The production and consumption of Mesoamerican tortillas underwent dramatic changes and made them global in the second half of the last century. The corn-tortilla production chain of grains, capital, and technologies crossed borders to satisfy North American appetites (Appendini, 2010). In the 1950s, the fields and laboratories of the US Midwest and later of the Mexico Central Plateau and Northern regions developed pollinated hybrid corn. In tandem, Mexican entrepreneurs created industrial-nixtamal instant flour and the mechanical tortilla maker, which yielded hundreds of tortillas in minutes. Commercial supermarkets in Monterrey, Guadalajara, Veracruz, and Mexico City gradually displaced traditional tortilla purveyors (Gómez-Galvarriato, 2022). Soon, urban groceries and supermarkets across North and Central America began selling tortillas; after the signing of the North American Free Trade Agreement, even consumers in South American capital cities could partake in *Maseca* or *Bimbo* tortillas.

Many foods that people had never eaten before were popularized after World War II or became ingredients in convenience foods. For instance, transnational companies turned vegetable oils (corn, palm, and soybean) from decolonized economies into components of almost all processed animal and vegetal foods, frozen meals, baked goods, candies, sauces, salad dressings, powdered milk,

---

[50] Nan Ickeringill, "The Freeze Is in on Europe: Minor Revolution Seen in the Frozen Foods," *The New York Times*, August 1, 1961.
[51] "Brand Pre-packing of Meats Forecast," *The New York Times*, April 25, 1953.

sausages, and ham, and bouillon cubes – a feature of recipes worldwide. The growth of the poultry industry illustrates this interplay among transnational agrifood systems, local-global supply channels, and the rise of protein-based urban diets. In the United States, vertical integration lowered feeding costs and delivered a faster-growing, heavier bird – the average chicken in the 1990s was twice as large as its 1930s counterpart – whose meat was, indeed, more affordable (Striffler, 2007). From the 1960s to the early 2000s, annual per capita chicken consumption tripled in the country. In 1960s European cities, poultry eating was a luxury; two decades later, frozen chicken prepared by working women became typical fare at dinner tables in Swiss cities and in urban Britain.[52] In the latter, by 1980 "technological chicken" made up a quarter of the total share of animal protein on the British table (Godley & Williams, 2009: 267). Technological chicken – fed with fishmeal, enhanced with antibiotics and growth hormones, and dressed in processing plants – and its iterations became standard fare everywhere. In 1950s Mexico City, the poultry industry development and household electrification made chicken an indispensable food at the Mexican urban table. Supermarkets and poultry shops (see Figure 10) offered "young chicken" (*pollos de leche*), dressed, chilled, or frozen, inexpensive birds (Matute Aguirre, 2006: 173–74). Rotisseries in popular and posh neighborhoods sold takeout roast chicken that the consumer (short on time and money) repurposed into quick, hearty meals, like chilaquiles. At home, skilled cooks transformed broiler chicken into the star ingredient of broths and tacos and central in traditional dishes, such as *Mexican mole*. Finally, chicken and egg consumption led Mexico's protein-based dietary transition. In Brazil, currently one of the world's leading chicken exporters, total annual poultry meat intake jumped from less than two kilos per person in 1961 to almost fifty in 1997. In 2010, São Paulo, Mexico City, and Hong Kong figured among the highest per capita consumers of chicken meat globally.

Another new food on almost every table worldwide was instant coffee. Brazilian and Mexican megacities were crucial in transforming the coffee supply chain. Since mid-1960s Mexico, where broadcasting television delivered shared experiences to millions of city dwellers, TV Telesistema Mexicano (in 1973, Televisa) aired "Your Nescafé News" (*Noticiero su diario Nescafé*) every morning. Alongside the news bulletin, Televisa advertised Nescafé instant coffee to approximately four million viewers (González de Bustamante, 2015: 176, 187). Before World War II, Nestlé technicians used Brazilian coffee beans and adapted "the spray-drying technology being used to

---

[52] Nan Ickeringill, "The Freeze Is in on Europe: Minor Revolution Seen in the Frozen Foods," *The New York Times*, August 1, 1961.

Figure 10 Expendio de pollo en el interior del mercado de Jamaica (Chicken
Sales in the Jamaica Market), Mexico City, 1960.

Source: Colección Nacho López, Fototeca Nacional, Instituto Nacional de Antropología
e Historia, Mexico City.

produce powdered milk... to make powdered instant coffee" (Talbot, 1997:
120). After the war, "Robusta" beans from decolonized Africa and South Asia
contributed to coffee innovations by Nestlé and other multinational corporations. Brazil and Mexico also developed their soluble coffee brands, which
urban (and rural) Mexican consumers could find in any CONASUPO store.
Alongside the enduring tradition of coffee house culture in Brazilian cities, as
shown in Figure 11, Brazil's instant coffee exports shaped this beverage's
consumption among urbanites in the Southern Cone.[53]

After the 1960s, massive food advertising in newspapers, radio, and television targeted children, youth, and female consumers, refashioning the eating
habits of all ages. As new, affordable, processed meals and dishes filled

---

[53] "13 datos clave para conocer la economía detrás del café," *Expansión* (Mexico City), October 1,
2022.

Figure 11 Cafezinho. Largo do Paissandu 1954 (circa), São Paulo, Alice Brill.
Source: Arquivo Alice Brill, Instituto Moreira Salles, Rio de Janeiro.

supermarkets' shelves and urban tables worldwide,[54] consumer preference for industrial food and national and global trademarks increased. Consider the case of breakfast cereal in Mexico City; as early as 1930, a newspaper advertised "Kellogg's Corn Flakes for lunch, good mom!" (Matute Aguirre, 2006: 172). Urban mass-eating culture (superposed on national food) connected urban residents everywhere. Today, in Mexico City's Zócalo (main plaza), urbanites celebrate the country's Independence Day, "screaming patriotic chants of 'Viva Mexico' ... drink[ing] Coca-Cola and eat[ing] hamburgers from a local McDonald's" (Moreno, 2011: 18).

Industrial and processed food challenged traditional eating habits and transformed urban meals at home and in the streets of Rio de Janeiro, Rome, Bagdad, New Delhi, Bombay, and Jakarta.[55] The supermarket expansion was essential to those adjustments, most notably because its model proved to be resilient,

---

[54] "Food Chains Plan World Convention," *The New York Times*, October 20, 1957.
[55] James J. Nagle, "General Foods Describe 'Benign Revolution in Kitchen'," *The New York Times*, September 12, 1962.

adapting to diverse contexts and expectations. In the 1980s, when the search for "natural foods" became mainstream, US supermarkets fought against their association with processed, unhealthy food; urban and suburban stores eliminated vertical aisle layouts and adopted farmer's market themes and appearance (Tinsman, 2014: 117–18). They also became purposefully "global," offering prepared food (sushi and burritos), specialty foods (gourmet coffee and cheese), and healthy staples (quinoa) and produce (avocados). Despite technology and diversified and abundant food offerings, urbanities' access to basic food remains unequal, politically charged, and highly contested.

Seeking Equitable Food Access in Prosperous Cities

In the latter decades of the past century, market liberalization drastically transformed cities' economic and social makeup, upending the livelihood of the poorest. In the Global South, the 1960s accelerated urbanization increasingly produced segregated metropolises (in services, infrastructure, health, education, and consumption patterns). Impoverished rural people who moved to cities seeking new opportunities settled in the surrounding areas and hills of modern Caracas, Rio de Janeiro, Lima, Santiago de Chile, Buenos Aires, Mexico City, or Brasília, creating entire communities with no permanent waged labor or access to infrastructure and services. Founded in 1960, Brasília – whose construction relied on spectacular engineering and urban planning – was meant to, among other factors, correct such inequalities. Yet disparities persisted in Brazil's new capital city and other metropolises worldwide; Cairo, Dakar, Bombay, and Istanbul had similar pockets of poverty. In Bogotá's "Barrio of 65," "hunger and pain are facts of every day."[56]

In the recent entangled history of cities and food, where supermarket chains had not entered, when food was unaffordable, and the state absent, consumer collectives proved vital to urban dwellers' struggles for citizenship, democracy, and food access. During the global privatization frenzy of the 1970s and 1980s, when the state was unable (or unwilling) to tackle hunger, collective organizations for food equity and alternative social welfare emerged everywhere. Canadian capital cities, facing de-industrialization in the early 1980s, witnessed the expansion of food banks that fed approximately 2.5 million people in 1994 (Riches, 1997: 67). In 1984–85, striking miners and their wives across England organized food collection and soup kitchens, which proved essential to families without income or benefits. In 1978 Lima, women from poor barrios created the city's first self-managed soup kitchens, a collective reaction against

---

[56] Sam Schulman, "Latin America Shanty-Town," *The New York Times*, January 16, 1966.

hyperinflation that left thousands at risk of starvation.[57] Amid the Shining Path's (*Sendero Luminoso* guerrilla) intimidation, and despite the state's attempts at cooptation and repression, these soup kitchens multiplied in Lima. By 1991, they distributed more than half a million rations daily, at a cost or free (Blondet & Montero, 1995: 83, 94). In Santiago de Chile, in the last years of Augusto Pinochet's dictatorship (1974–90), women and entire families organized cooperatives to confront multiple crises. They created people's kitchens (*ollas populares*), providing essential food to their communities during rampant unemployment and inflation. In 1982, more than one hundred ollas populares operated across the city without support from municipal or national governments (Hardy, 1986: 33).

Subsistence revolts that incubated political democratic demands spread across capital cities worldwide. In 1977 Cairo, people took to the streets in the so-called International Monetary Fund riots, protesting bread subsidy elimination.[58] These uprisings represented a milestone in public discussion about social rights to include waged workers, informal laborers, and the poorest (Serulnikov, 2017). In the severe economic crises of the 1980s–2000s, which, unlike the 1930s debacle, affected only the Global South, many Latin American countries lost two decades of growth and comprehensive social development; jobs and state-funded benefits disappeared while rampant inflation eroded any wage gains. Residents in São Paulo and other Latin American urban centers faced hyperinflation and meat, rice, and coffee shortages. In Caracas, soaring food and fuel prices triggered the social revolt *Caracazo* from February to March 1989, a turning point in Venezuelan history (López Maya, 2003). In May, citizens in Buenos Aires, Rosario, and Córdoba looted local retailers and supermarkets. Women and children took bread, pasta, cheese, yogurt, milk, and meat – whose prices had risen between 550 percent and 1,000 percent (depending on the product) in only four months.

In the 1990s, the collapse of the Soviet Union and other socialist regimes revived dramatic memories of wartime scarcity and contrasted with the abundance-euphoria urbanities in the eastern bloc experienced a decade earlier. The latter taught consumers to be activists in buying and complaining (Chernyshova, 2013: 203). Because the state was the only legitimate food purveyor, citizens readily identified those in power with price hikes and shortages. In Lodz, a Polish industrial city, and Warsaw, state provisions could not placate scarcity, and food rationing was imposed in 1976. In the summer of 1981, when the government reduced meat provisions, 50,000

---

[57] "Study Details Socioeconomic Levels in Lima," *Peru Económico*, February 1992.

[58] Michael Slackman, "Bread, the (Subsidized) Stuff of Life in Egypt," *The New York Times*, January 16, 2008.

women and children marched through Lodz's streets; "The March against Hunger" denounced the unfair and inefficient rationing system (Mazurek & Clavier, 2013). In Warsaw, the Solidarity union galvanized the masses with strikes and protests that paralyzed the city.[59]

Significantly, the aforementioned crises reframed people's citizenship in connection to their social and urban settings rather than to political parties or trade unions (Serulnikov, 2017). By strengthening their communal links, impoverished people also repurposed urban spaces and gardens. Over the last century, from the 1914 War Garden to the Great Depression Relief Garden and the World War II Victory Garden, or urban dachas across the Soviet Union, men and women transformed vacant land into cultivated fields, providing work to the unemployed and foodstuffs to their families. The urban green belt around Havana that 1960s revolutionaries envisioned feeding Cuba's capital city reemerged after the Soviet Union collapsed, supplying vegetables and herbs to city residents and jobs to displaced workers (Oliveira, 2017: 61). In 2001, 47 percent of urban households in Russian cities grew some food. Post-Soviet urban agriculture had contradictory and conflicting meanings. In capitalist Russia, citizens who engaged in dacha food production challenged commercial retail; those who rejected it adopted market-oriented behavior to reinforce their class status (Zavisca, 2003).

Urban and peri-urban agriculture have always been integral to urban economies, as demonstrated in previous sections. In Mexico City, less than 30 kilometers from the metropolis's political center, peasant communities still use floating gardens to harvest corn, spinach, tomatoes, lettuce, carrots, aromatic and medicinal herbs, and ornamental plants.[60] Urban agriculture might have played a pivotal role in alleviating urban poverty; in 1990, Buenos Aires residents who tended their gardens for less than two days weekly shaved off between 10 percent and 30 percent of their food bill. In poor neighborhoods, that amount equated to an income increase between 5 percent and 20 percent.[61] According to a Food and Agriculture Organization of the United Nations (FAO) report, in the 1990s, urban farming had become a significant source of fresh food provision in Katmandu, Hong Kong, Karachi, and Shanghai. Since the 1980s, Beijing's suburban grounds and greenhouses have regularly supplied farm produce to its inhabitants (Parham, 2015: 191). Rapid demographic

---

[59] "Crece la tensión social en Polonia como consecuencia de la escasez de alimentos," *El País* (Madrid), July 29, 1981.

[60] José Genovevo Pérez Espinosa, "Pueblos chinamperos de la Ciudad de México," *La Jornada del campo* (Mexico City), no. 32, May 22, 2010.

[61] FAO, *The State of Food and Agriculture: Food Security: Some Macroeconomic Dimensions*, Rome, 1996.

expansion in African cities led to significantly unequal environments, with families adopting various strategies to secure food. By the 1990s, between 25 and 85 percent of metropolitan areas in the continent had access to urban farming.[62] Such variation speaks to the limitations of this type of agriculture. In Kenyan and Zambian metropolises today, medium-income households are more likely to engage in urban farming partly because poor inhabitants lack space, time, and resources (Davies *et al.*, 2021; Lee-Smith, 2010). Recently, city agriculture proved fundamental in the Global North, as Milwaukee (Wisconsin) and other towns in the United States and Canada experienced deindustrialization and emerging pockets of poverty (Riches, 1997).

Urban centers in the age of globalization witnessed various and successive changes in food supply chains, distribution, and marketing. As elucidated in this discussion, these changes went hand in hand with new urban social realities and the growth of spatially and socioeconomically segregated cities. Attuned to these shifts, metropolises in the Global South, such as Cairo and Mexico City, developed food supply infrastructures capable of coordinating large-scale deliveries from nearby rural areas, world markets, and transnational corporations. Central de Abasto in Mexico City, built in the 1970s (inaugurated in 1982), was emblematic of this trend. Concurrently, municipalities and private capital developed central wholesale facilities to marshal strategic food reserves within and between cities. In Quito, La Paz (Bolivia), and Colombian cities, governments created distribution corridors, linking farmers to small vendors in urban areas (Meyer, 1999, 71).

In other metropolitan centers, these broad transformations entailed relocating public markets to the city outskirts or redesigning ancient structures to house shopping malls. Although depilated, these symbols of fin-de-siècle modernity sat on valued real estate that was privatized and refurbished. These were cases of Georges Pompidou Cultural Center, near Les Halles in Paris, and in Buenos Aires, the Spinetto Shopping (originally Spinetto fresh products market, founded in the 1890s). London's Covent Garden, Madrid's Mercado de San Miguel, and Buenos Aires's Mercado de Abasto Proveedor underwent similar makeovers to sell gourmet products and foods to affluent clientele and tourists (Sassano, 2001). The new public market infrastructure built in Barcelona was paradigmatic of yet another change in retail, the rise of "ethnic" foods. The city council built *Mercabarna*, the largest wholesale market of fresh goods in the Mediterranean region. It also renovated city markets and promoted small retail in neighborhoods. Under municipal

---

[62] Ibid.

supervision, local commerce recovered, offering food of Indian, Pakistani, South American, Mexican, and Vietnamese origin.

Concurrently, the eating-out phenomenon reached a zenith worldwide. In the 1990s, Beijing, Tianjin, and Shanghai residents saw an exponential increase in Western fast-food outlets. In 1992, weeks after the opening of McDonald's in Beijing, a traditional Chinese restaurant in proximity closed its doors, "in its stead opened International Fast-Food City, which sold Japanese food, American hamburgers, fried chicken and ice cream" (Yan, 2000: 205). Customers flocked to relish these new foods, a striking departure from a few decades earlier, when most residents ate at their homes or workplace canteens. At the same time, in Russian urban centers, McDonald's opened its doors to an avid consumer despite prices. These events speak of status eating associated with winners and losers of the Cold War, the globalization of tastes, and the ethnic food phenomenon. In the 1990s, as Muscovites queued for hours to savor Big Macs, Londoners enjoyed more "global dishes" than any other consumer in Great Britain; ethnic food is today a feature of supermarkets, restaurants, and street food. The latter has come full circle, enjoying a prominence it did not have in the early 1900s. On the heels of the 2008 Great Recession, food trucks popped up in urban centers worldwide; bringing gourmet foods and their cooks outside restaurants, they created new spaces for leisure associated with eating for the middle- and upper-class. As this Element has examined, in the early 1900s, street eating was inextricable to the urban experience of migrants and working-class urbanities, who prepared and ate that food. Today, local authorities and passersby seem more empathetic to these latest street-eating iterations than their counterparts were to poor vendors in the early twentieth century, revealing contested notions about who has the right to occupy cities' spaces and with what purpose.

In the last century, supermarkets revolutionized cities' food provision, linking transnational agribusiness to urbanites' tables, and shaping diets. Supermarkets did not reach every city corner, nor did they plow out other forms of retail; if anything, as this section shows, they proved highly capable of reinventing themselves, adapting to different political and economic regimes and consumer preferences. The latter, nonetheless, remains elusive, as metropolises today may be as segregated (or even more) as they were a century ago; in fact, poor and rich may never cross paths, not even to buy or eat food in their cities' public spaces.

Conclusion

Urban foodways underwent dramatic transformations from the 1880s to 2010, an era shaped by revolutions, wars, economic fluctuation, and the strengthening of capitalism. Central to this Element's narrative is the intertwined dynamic of globalization and urbanization. Both shaped how city dwellers accessed and interacted with food and navigated a complex interplay of natural forces and market influences. Scientific innovations, capital flows, and industrialization connected urban food systems with translocal and global factors. In response to these shifts, over the century, municipal authorities and bureaucracies in large cities embarked on various experiments in social engineering, food policy planning, and initiatives aimed at dietary enhancement. In the early 1900s, the ties between food and its place of origin began to loosen. Agribusiness conglomerates and financial networks have since orchestrated food circulation on a global scale, spanning production sites to consumption hubs across regions, oceans, and continents. Today's global commodity chains facilitate the journey of avocados harvested in Latin America and cod caught in the Baltic Sea to bistros and shops in cities across Europe and Africa. Despite the extensive transnational connections in urban supply chains, domestic systems also play a crucial role in providing diverse food to urban centers. Regional farmers continue to supply fruits and vegetables to cities' street markets, maintaining a vital link to local produce. Similarly, urban agriculture persists as a cornerstone of city diets worldwide. Given these dynamics, it is pertinent to consider whether, in the forthcoming decades, the environmental and sustainability challenges facing metropolises will foster the growth of local, peri-urban, and intra-urban provision models.

Since the advent of capitalism and the modern city, residents of diverse backgrounds have obtained their food in public and open-air markets, grocery stores, bakeries, and butcher shops, among other establishments. These venues intersected with social consumption dynamics in public spaces, from street vendors to workplace cafeterias, retail outlets, cafes, communal kitchens, and restaurants. Despite retail innovation, traditional corner stores and street selling endured during the past century, supplying neighborhoods and outlying residential areas. This Element underscores the significant disruption brought about by supermarkets in urban food systems. Commercial supermarkets have remarkably adapted to various productive, urban, and socio-demographic contexts worldwide; as they multiplied, consumers wielded agency over these establishments' offerings, pricing, and sale conditions, a phenomenon observed in capitalist and socialist economies. Supermarkets also facilitated the offering of more diverse raw, processed, and prepared foods; concurrently urban diets homogenized around the intake of animal proteins, processed foods, flours, and sugars. This Element also considers countervailing tendencies to global forces, for instance, when locals rejected migrants' foodways, selectively evoking national culinary traditions.

In this work, food inequality emerges as a defining feature of the urban experience. In the late nineteenth century, large cities seemed to provide better food prospects to displaced peasants and migrants than the countryside, marking a clear distinction in food access between rural and urban spaces. However, intra-urban inequalities have deepened over the past century, erasing such dichotomies. Another focal point of analysis in this Element is the socially constructed and negotiated nature of food consumption. On various occasions, urban consumers organized to defend their right to access reasonably priced, safe food, even within the constraints of socialist economies. The study investigates the emergence of the modern consumer and their evolving expectations and avenues of action. Initially rooted in local communities, consumer activism eventually transcended national boundaries to encompass transnational coordinated efforts. Examples abound, from collective mobilization against hunger in crisis-ridden cities across the Global South to international debates within organizations advocating for food health and safety standards and public campaigns challenging the dominance of food industry corporations.

This Element stresses the profound transformation in domestic life within the food realm. In a gradual and far-reaching progression, market forces and industrialization altered the time spent grocery shopping and cooking and fundamentally reshaped the dynamics between genders and children rearing. Mothers and their offspring, central figures in this Element, now consume processed foods that were nonexistent a century ago. Audiovisual and digital advertising networks – and public incentives – promoted these products and made them widely available.

Despite the remarkable advancements in agrifood technologies, the foundational elements of the human diet in the twenty-first century remain rooted in plants, animals, and their industrialized derivatives. Global megalopolises today, akin to imperial capitals just before World War I, still depend on the labor and resources of rural expanses on other continents. While urban consumers strive to safeguard their purchasing power for essential foods amid inflation, shortages, and market fluctuations, local growers grapple – much like their counterparts a century ago – with global commodity chains that threaten their livelihoods. Putting food on the dinner table remains a concern for both parties.

References

Adell, I. H. & Pujol, J. (2017). Cities and Milk Consumption in Europe, 1890–1936: The Emergence of a New Market in Spain. *Historia Agraria*, 73, 59–89.

Aldous, C. (2013). A Dearth of Animal Protein: Reforming Nutrition in Occupied Japan (1945–1952). In K. J. Cwiertka, ed., *Food and War in Mid-Twentieth-Century East Asia*. Burlington: Ashgate, pp. 53–72.

Appendini, K. (2010). *La integración regional de la cadena maíz-tortilla*. Documentos de investigación, 3 Colección TLCAN, COLMEX.

Arellano Ramírez, F. A. (2020). Mercados en la ciudad de México: espacio, reforma urbana y conflicto político (1946–1957), MA thesis, UNAM.

Asfaw, A. (2008). Does Supermarket Purchase Affect the Dietary Practices of Households? Some Empirical Evidence from Guatemala. *Development Policy Review*, 26(2), 227–43.

Barrán, J. P. & Nahum, B. (1984). Las clases populares en el Montevideo del novecientos. In J. P. Barrán, ed., *Sectores populares y vida urbana*. Buenos Aires: CLACSO, pp. 11–36.

Battersby, J. & Peyton, S. (2014). The Geography of Supermarkets in Cape Town: Supermarket Expansion and Food Access. *Urban Forum*, 25, 153–64.

Berdahl, D. (1999). *Where the World Ended: Re-unification and Identity in the German Borderland*. Berkeley: University of California Press.

Bergère, M. C. (1973). Une Crise de Subsistance en Chine (1920–1922). *Annales. Économies, Sociétés, Civilisations*, 28(6), 1361–402.

Bergère, M. C. (2017). *Shanghai: China's Gateway to Modernity*. Stanford: Stanford University Press.

Berghoff, H. (2017). Consumption on the Home Front during the Second World War: A Transnational Perspective. In H. Berghoff, J. Logemann, and F. Römer, eds., *The Consumer on the Home Front: Second World War Civilian Consumption in Comparative Perspective*. Oxford: Oxford University Press, pp. 3–25.

Bidlack, R. & Lomagin, N. (2012). *The Leningrad Blockade, 1941–1944: A New Documentary History from the Soviet Archives*. New Heaven: Yale University Press.

Bleynat, I. (2021). *Vendors' Capitalism: A Political Economy of Public Markets in Mexico City*. Stanford: Stanford University Press.

Blondet, C. & Montero, C. (1995). *Hoy: Menu popular. Comedores de Lima*. Lima: Instituto de Estudios Peruanos, UNICEF.

Bobrow-Strain, A. (2011). Making White Bread by the Bomb's Early Light: Anxiety, Abundance, and Industrial Food Power in the Early Cold War. *Food and Foodways*, 19(1), 74–97.

Bonzon, T. & Davis, B. (2007). Feeding the Cities. In R. Jean-Lous and J. Winter, eds., *Capital Cities at War Paris, London, Berlin 1914–1919*. Cambridge: Cambridge University Press, pp. 305–41.

Bruegel, M. (2015). Workers Lunch Away from Home in the Paris of the Belle Epoque: The French Model of Meals as Norm and Practice. *French Historical Studies*, 38(2), 253–80.

Campos Posada, A. (2020). La batalla del hambre: el abastecimiento de Madrid durante la Guerra Civil (1936–1939), PhD dissertation, Universidad Complutense de Madrid.

Cerutti, M. & Rivas Sada, E. (2006). El agro comercio como escalón a las grandes cadenas urbanas: Ángel Losada Gómez y la construcción del grupo Gigante (1923–2004). In R. Domínguez and M. Cerutti, eds., *De la colonia a la globalización: empresarios cántabros en México*. Santander: Universidad de Cantabria, 261–81.

Chen, Y. (2017). The Rise of Chinese Food in the United States. *Oxford Research Encyclopedia of American History*, [online]. (Accessed September 18, 2021), https://doi.org/10.1093/acrefore/9780199329175.013.273.

Chernyshova, N. (2013). *Soviet Consumer Culture in the Brezhnev Era*. New York: Routledge.

Cheung, G. C. K. & Gomez, E. T. (2012). Hong Kong's Diaspora, Networks, and Family Business in the United Kingdom: A History of the Chinese "Food Chain" and the Case of W. Wing Yip Group. *The China Review*, 12(1), 45–72.

Claflyn, K. & Scholliers, P. (2012). *Writing Food History: A Global Perspective*. London: Berg.

Clarence-Smith, W. G. & Topik, S. (2003). Introduction: Coffee and Global Development. In W. G. Clarence-Smith and S. Topik, eds., *The Global Coffee Economy in Africa, Asia, and Latin America, 1500–1989*. Cambridge: Cambridge University Press, pp. 1–20.

Collingham, L. (2012). *The Taste of War*. New York: The Penguin Press.

Couto, C. L. M. & Alfonso-Goldfarb, A. M. (2016). A Cup o'controversy: Coffee and Health in 19th Century Rio de Janeiro. *Circumscribere: International Journal for the History of Science*, 17, 41–53.

Crush, J. & Frayne, B. (2011). Supermarket Expansion and the Informal Food Economy in Southern African Cities: Implications for Urban Food Security. *Journal of Southern African Studies*, 37(4), 781–807.

Czaplicki, A. (2007). "Pure Milk Is Better than Purified Milk": Pasteurization and Milk Purity in Chicago, 1908–1916. *Social Science History*, 31(3), 411–33.

Davies, J., Hannah, C., Guido, Z., *et al.* (2021). Barriers to Urban Agriculture in Sub-Saharan Africa. *Food Policy*, 103, 1–14.

Dietrich, A. (2020). Oranges and the New Black: Importing, Provisioning, and Consuming Tropical Fruits and Coffee in the GDR, 1971–1981. In C. Scarboro, D. Mincyte, and Z. Gille, eds., *The Socialist Good Life Desire, Development, and Standards of Living in Eastern Europe*. Bloomington: Indiana University Press, pp. 104–31.

Drinot, P. (2005). Food, Race and Working-Class Identity: *Restaurantes Populares* and Populism in 1930s Peru. *The Americas*, 62(2), 245–70.

Dufour, S. (1671). De l'usage du café, du thé et du chocolaté, A Lyon, chez Jean Girin, & Barthelemy Rivière, en rué Mercière, à la Prudence. M.DC. LXXI. Avec permission des supérieurs.

Durr, K. D. (2006). *A Company with a Mission: Rodman Rockefeller and the International Basic Economic Corporation, 1947–1985*. Rockville: Montrose Press.

Elena, E. (2007). Peronist Consumer Politics and the Problem of Domesticating Markets in Argentina, 1943–1955. *Hispanic American Historical Review*, 87(1), 111–49.

Eliot, M. M. & Heseltine, M. M. (1937). Nutrition Studies of the League of Nations and the International Labour Office Geneva, 1936. *Social Service Review* 11(2), 331–34.

Fawcett, W. (1921). *The Banana: Its Cultivation, Distribution, and Commercial Uses*. London: Duckworth and Co.

Figuié, M. & Moustier, P. (2009). Market Appeal in an Emerging Economy: Supermarkets and Poor Consumers in Vietnam. *Food Policy*, 34(2), 210–17.

Fogagnoli, M. M. (2011). *"Almoçar bem é no SAPS!"*: os trabalhadores e o Serviço de Alimentação da Previdência Social (1940–1950), PhD dissertation, Universidade Federal Fluminense.

Francks, P. (2015). Rice and the Path of Economic Development in Japan. In F. Bray, P., Coclanis, E. Fields-Black, D. Schäfer, eds., *Rice: Global Networks and New Histories*. New York: Cambridge University Press, pp. 318–34.

Frens-String, J. (2021). *Hungry for Revolution: The Politics of Food and the Making of Modern Chile*. Oakland: University of California Press.

Fu, J. C. (2018). *The Other Milk: Reinventing Soy in Republican China*. Seattle: University of Washington Press.

Garon, S. (2017). The Home Front and Food Insecurity in Wartime Japan: A Transnational Perspective. In H. Berghoff, J. Logemann, and F. Römer, eds., *The Consumer on the Home Front: Second World War Civilian Consumption in Comparative Perspective*. Oxford: Oxford University Press, pp. 29–53.

Garrido, C. (2020). Mujeres trabajadoras en la provincia de La Habana. Identidades, marcas de subalternidad y cultura obrera de las despalilladoras de tabaco, 1898–1948, PhD dissertation, El Colegio de México.

Garvin, D. (2023). Fruit of Fascist Empire: Bananas and Italian Somaliland. *The Italianist*, 43(3), 439–67, https://doi.org/10.1080/02614340.2023.2257943.

Gayol, S. (2000). *Sociabilidad en Buenos Aires: Hombres, honor y cafés 1862–1910*. Buenos Aires: Editorial del Signo.

Godley, A. & Williams, B. (2009). Democratizing Luxury and the Contentious "Invention of the Technological Chicken" in Britain. *Business History Review*, 83, 267–90.

Goldman, W. Z. & Filtzer, D. A. (2021). *Fortress Dark and Stern: The Soviet Home Front during World War II*. New York: Oxford University Press.

Gómez, F. & Zubizarreta, I. (2015). Producción y comercialización de la leche en Buenos Aires y su hinterland durante la incipiente industrialización del sector lácteo (1880–1910). In A. Lluch, ed., *Las manos visibles del mercado: Intermediarios y consumidores en la Argentina*. Rosario: Prohistoria, pp. 71–88.

Gómez-Galvarriato, A. (2022). La industrialización del nixtamal y la elaboración de la tortilla en México. *RIRA*, 7(1), 231–74.

González de Bustamante, C. (2015). *Muy buenas noches: México, la televisión y la Guerra Fría*. México: Fondo de Cultura Económica.

González Pizarro, J. A. (1999). Las estrategias económicas regionales en la década de 1930 en Antofagasta. *Revista de Ciencias Sociales*, 9, 20–40.

Goudeau, É. (1893). *Paris qui consomme: tableaux de Paris* / Emile Goudeau; dessins de Pierre Vidal, https://gallica.bnf.fr/ark:/12148/bpt6k1521949k.

Graf, K. (2018). Cereal Citizens: Crafting Bread and Belonging in Urbanizing Morocco. *Paideuma*, 64, 227–44.

Graziosi, A. (2017). Political Famine in the USRR and China: A Comparative Analysis. *Journal of Cold War Studies*, 19(3), 42–103.

Grossman, J. R. (1989). *Land of Hope: Chicago, Black Southerners, and the Great Migration*. Chicago: University of Chicago Press.

Guerrero Cantarell, R. (2019). Lovely Bananas! An Exploration of the Banana Trade in Sweden 1906–1939. *History of Retailing and Consumption*, 6(1), 5–29.

Gutiérrez Rueda, C. & Gutiérrez Rueda, L. (2015). *El hambre en Madrid de la Guerra Civil, 1936–1937*. Madrid: Ediciones La Librería.

Hale-Dorrell, A. (2015). Industrial Farming, Industrial Food: Transnational Influences on Soviet Convenience Food in the Khrushchev Era. *The Soviet and Post-Soviet Review*, 42(2), 174–196.

Hale-Dorrell, A. T. (2014). Khrushchev's Corn Crusade: The Industrial Ideal and Agricultural Practice in the Era of Post-Stalin Reform, 1953–1964, PhD dissertation, University of North Carolina.

Hamilton, S. (2018). *Supermarket USA: Food and Power in the Cold War Farms Race*. New Haven: Yale University Press.

Harada, M. (2016). Japanese Modern Municipal Retail and Wholesale Markets in Comparison with European Markets. *Urban History*, 43(3), 476–92.

Hardy, C. (1986). *Hambre + Dignidad = Ollas Comunes*. Santiago: PET.

Hawkes, C. (2008). Dietary Implications of Supermarket Development: A Global Perspective. *Development Policy Review*, 26(6), 657–92.

Helguera, D. (1893). *La producción argentina en 1892, descripción de la industria nacional; su desarrollo y progreso en toda la República*, Buenos Aires: Editores Goyoaga y Cía., 4, 39.

Jacobs, A. K. (2019). Love, Marry, Cook: Gendering the Home Kitchen in Late Soviet Russia. In A. Lakhtikova, A. Brintlinger, and I. Glushchenko, eds. *Seasoned Socialism: Gender and Food in Late Soviet Everyday Life*. Bloomington: Indiana University Press.

Jacobs, M. (1997). "How about Some Meat?": The Office of Price Administration, Consumption Politics, and State Building from the Bottom Up, 1941–1946. *The Journal of American History*, 84(3), 910–41.

Joseph, S. C. (1961). *Food Policy and Economic Development in India, Bombay, Calcutta, New Delhi, Madras*. Delhi: Allied.

Kelley, V. (2016). The Streets for the People: London's Street Markets, 1850–1939. *Urban History*, 43(3), 391–411.

Klarén, P. F. (1986). The Origins of Modern Peru, 1880–1930. In L. Bethell, ed., *The Cambridge History of Latin America*. Part 4. Cambridge: Cambridge University Press, pp. 587–640.

Knecher, L. & Fuld, R. (1998). Orígenes, desarrollo y desaparición de una empresa de capital nacional: la historia de Kasdorf S. A. *Ciclos*, 8(16), 163–90.

Lee, R. (2006). Heart and Home in Cape Town: African Women, Energy Resourcing, and Consumption in an Urban Environment. *Journal of Women's History*, 18(4), 55–78.

Lee-Smith, D. (2010). Cities Feeding People: An Update on Urban Agriculture in Equatorial Africa. *Environment & Urbanization*, 22(2), 483–99.

Leong-Salobir, C. (2015). *Mem y Cookie*: la cocina colonial en Malasia y Singapur. *Estudios de Asia y Africa*, 50(3), 621–50.

Levenstein, H. A. (2003). *Paradox of Plenty: A Social History of Eating in Modern America*. Berkeley: University of California Press.

Liao, C., Tan, Y., Wu, C., *et al.* (2016). City Level of Income and Urbanization and Availability of Food Stores and Food Service Places in China. *PLoS ONE*, 11(3), 1–12.

Lluch, A. (2015). Del campo a la mesa: comercialización de carnes en la Argentina: actores, mercados y políticas de regulación (1895c–1930). In A. Lluch, ed., *Las manos visibles del mercado: intermediarios y consumidores en la Argentina.* Rosario: Prohistoria, pp. 89–120.

Lock Reyna, M. (2006). De la tiendita al supermercado: los comerciantes chinos en América Latina y el Caribe. *Nueva Sociedad*, 203, 128–37.

López Maya, M. (2003). The Venezuelan *Caracazo* of 1989: Popular Protest and Institutional Weakness. *Journal of Latin American Studies*, 35(1), 117–37.

Masterovoy, A. (2013). *Eating Soviet: Food and Culture in the USSR, 1917– 1991*, PhD dissertation, The City University of New York.

Masterovoy, A. (2017). What Was Socialist Food and What Comes Next? *Contemporary European History*, 26(3), 523–32.

Matocq, E. (1944). *Bases para el ordenamiento del Mercado de Carnes en la ciudad de Buenos Aires*, PhD dissertation, Universidad de Buenos Aires.

Matos, M. I. de S. (2009). Portugueses e experiências políticas: a luta e o pão: São Paulo 1870–1945. *História, São Paulo*, 28(1), 415–43.

Matute Aguirre, A. (2006). De la tecnología al orden doméstico en el México de la posguerra. In A. De los Reyes, ed., *Historia de la vida cotidiana en México. V-2. Siglo XX. La imagen ¿espejo de la vida?* México: El Colegio de México, Fondo de Cultura Económica, pp. 157–76.

Mazurek, M. & Clavier, A. (2013). Morales de la consommation en Pologne (1918–1989). *Annales. Histoire, Sciences Sociales*, (avril-juin) 68(2), Le quotidien du communisme, 499–527.

McCaa, R. (2003). Missing Millions: The Demographic Costs of the Mexican Revolution. *Mexican Studies/Estudios Mexicanos*, 19(2), 367–400.

McCall, J. (1910). Fruit Production of the British Empire. *Journal of the Royal Society of Arts*, 58 (2992), 475–485.

McFarland, S. (1985). Anatomy of an Iranian Political Crowd: The Tehran Bread Riot of December 1942. *International Journal of Middle East Studies*, 17(1), 51–65.

Meyer, M. D. (1999). Urban Food Diversity and Cost Variability in Caracas, Venezuela, 1988–97: A Neighborhood Provision Study, PhD dissertation, Indiana State University.

Milanesio, N. (2014). *Cuando los trabajadores salieron de compras: nuevos consumidores, publicidad y cambio cultural durante el primer peronismo.* Buenos Aires: Siglo XXI Editores.

Mintz, S. W. (1996). *Dulzura y poder: el lugar del azúcar en la historia moderna*. México: Siglo XXI Editores.

Mitsuda, T. (2024). From Colonial Hoof to Metropolitan Table: The Imperial Biopolitics of Beef Provisioning in Colonial Korea. *Global Food History*, 10(1), 8–27.

Morard III, D. (2023). Communist Quality: Dairy Production at the Leningrad Dairy Combine, 1965–1982. *Global Food History*, 1–20, https://www.tand fonline.com/doi/full/10.1080/20549547.2023.2249567.

Moreno, J. E. (2011). What Global Capitalism Leaves to the Nation: Coca Cola, the United States, and Latin America, *Research Gate*, https://www.researchgate.net/ publication/267516323_What_Global_Capitalism_Leaves_to_the_Nation_ Coca-Cola_the_United_States_and_Latin_America.

Mouré, K. (2010). Food Rationing and the Black Market in France (1940–1944). *French History*, 24(2), 268–84.

Muniz, É. S. (2018). Comida, ciência e trabalho: nutrição e assistência social no Serviço de Alimentação da Previdência Social (SAPS), 1940–1945. *Revista do Arquivo Geral da cidade do Rio de Janeiro*, 15, 187–207.

Neill, D. (2009). Finding the "Ideal Diet": Nutrition, Culture, and Dietary Practices in France and French Equatorial Africa, c. 1890s to 1920s. *Food and Foodways*, 17(1), 1–28.

Nilsen, M. (2014). *The Working Man's Green Space: Allotment Gardens In England, France, and Germany, 1870-1919*. Charlottesville: The University of Virginia Press.

Ocampo, J. A., Stallings, B., Bustillo, I., Velloso, H., and Frenkel, R. (2014). *La crisis latinoamericana de la deuda desde la perspectiva histórica*. Santiago de Chile: Naciones Unidas, CEPAL.

Ochoa, E. (2000). *Feeding Mexico: The Political Uses of Food since 1910*. Wilmington: Scholarly Resources.

Oliveira, L. C. P. de (2017). Redes, ideias e ação pública na agricultura urbana: São Paulo, Montreal e Toronto, PhD dissertation, Fundação Getúlio Vargas.

Parham, S. (2015). *Food and Urbanism: The Convivial City and Sustainable Future*. London: Bloomsbury.

Patterson, P. H. (2009). Making Markets Marxist? The East European Grocery Store from Rationing to Rationality to Rationalizations. In W. J. Belasco and R. Horowitz, eds. *Food Chains: From Farmyard to Shopping Cart*, Philadelphia: University of Pennsylvania Press.

Pence, C. (2012). Grounds for Discontent? Coffee from the Black Market to the Kafflekatsch in the GDR. In P. Bren and M. Neuburger, eds., *Communism*

Unwrapped: Consumption in Cold War Eastern Europe. Oxford: Oxford University Press, pp. 197–225.

Pérez Samper, M. de los Á. (2002). El pan nuestro de cada día en la Barcelona moderna. *Pedralbes: Revista d'historia moderna*, 22, 29–71.

Pilcher, J. M. (2012). *Planet Taco: A Global History of Mexican Food*. Oxford: Oxford University Press.

Pohl-Valero, S. (2016). Alimentación, raza, productividad y desarrollo: entre problemas sociales nacionales y políticas nutricionales internacionales, Colombia, 1890–1950. In G. Mateos and E. Suárez, eds., *Aproximaciones a lo local y lo global: América Latina en la historia de la ciencia contemporánea*. México: Centro de Estudios Filosóficos, Políticos y Sociales Vicente Lombardo Toledano, pp. 115–54.

Pollard, H. B. C. (1913). *A Busy Time in Mexico: An Unconventional Record of Mexican Incident*. New York: Duffield and Company.

Poppendieck, J. & Nestle M. (2014). *Breadlines Knee-Deep in Wheat: Food Assistance in the Great Depression*. Berkeley: University of California Press.

Porter, S. (2003). *Working Women in Mexico City: Public Discourses and Material Conditions, 1879–1931*. Tucson: University of Arizona Press.

Prakash, G. & Adelman, J. eds. (2023). *Inventing the Third World: In Search of Freedom for the Postwar Global South, Histories of Internationalism*. London: Bloomsbury Academic.

Pureco Ornelas, A. & García Crescencio, A. D. (2017). Del Estado al mercado. La tendencia general de la producción del arroz en México, 1930–2010. *Letras históricas*, 17, 157–83.

Ramírez Plancarte, F. (2016). *La Ciudad de México durante la Revolución Constitucionalista*. México: INHERM.

Ramírez Rodríguez, R. (2015). Contrapunteando a la cerveza y al pulque en la década de 1920: el origen del cambio de gustos en las bebidas nacionales. *Meyibó: Revista de Investigaciones Históricas*, 5(10), 97–110.

Ramsingh, B. L. N. (2011). The History of International Food Safety Standards and the Codex Alimentarius (1955–1995), PhD dissertation, University of Toronto.

Rapoport, M. & Lazzari, R. (2014). La Primera Guerra Mundial y el comercio de granos en la Argentina: Neutralidad y puja anglo-germana. *Revista de la Bolsa de Comercio de Rosario*, 38–44.

Rey, A. L. (2019). La divulgación del "buen comer" y las imágenes de la mesa de los sectores populares (1900–1930). *Confluenze: Rivista di Studi Iberoamericani*, XI (1), 56–76.

Reynolds, T. (2000). The Global Banana Trade. In S. Striffler and M. Moberg, eds., *Banana Wars: Power, Production, and History in the Americas.* Durham: Duke University Press, pp. 23–47.

Riches, G. (1997). Hunger, Food Security and Welfare Policies: Issues and Debates in First World Societies. *Proceedings of the Nutrition Society,* 56, 63–74.

Rodríguez Kuri, A. (2013). *Historia del desasosiego: la revolución en la ciudad de México, 1911–1922.* México: El Colegio de México.

Rodríguez Terrazas, I. (2001). Protesta y soberanía popular: Las marchas del hambre en Chile, BA thesis, Pontificia Universidad Católica de Chile.

Rude, M. (1877). *Tout-Paris au café.* Paris: Maurice Dreyfous Éditeur.

Ruiz Zevallos, A. (2001). *La multitud, las subsistencias y el trabajo: Lima, 1890–1990.* Lima: Pontificia Universidad Católica del Perú.

Salinas Sánchez, A. (2013). *Polos opuestos: salarios y costo de vida, 1821–1879.* Lima: Universidad Mayor de San Marcos, Seminario de Historia Rural Andina.

Sanghera, S. (2023). Empire of Tea, Podcast Series (1–10), BBC Radio 4. Retrieved from: https://www.bbc.co.uk/sounds/brand/m001t30b?partner=uk.co.bbc&origin=share-mobile.

Sarmiento Ramírez, I. (2002). La alimentación cubana, (1800–1868): sistema de abasto y comercialización. *Anales del Museo de América,* 10, 219–54.

Sassano, S. (2001). Transformación de un espacio urbano: el caso del Mercado de Abasto de Buenos Aires, *Anales de Geografía de la Universidad Complutense* 21, 99–118.

Sasson, T. (2016a). From Empire to Humanity: The Russian Famine and the Imperial Origins of International Humanitarianism. *Journal of British Studies,* 55(3), 519–37.

Sasson, T. (2016b). Milking the Third World? Humanitarianism, Capitalism, and the Moral Economy of the Nestlé Boycott. *The American Historical Review,* 121(4), 1196–224.

Schewe, E. (2017). How War Shaped "Egypt's National Bread Loaf." *Comparative Studies of South Asia, Africa and the Middle East,* 37(1), 49–63.

Schoenholt, D. N. (2018). Coca-Cola's History in Coffee: Though Coca-Cola's Acquisition of Costa Coffee Surprised Many, the Soft Drink Giant Has a Long History in the Coffee Industry. *The Tea & Coffee Trade Journal,* 190(10), 36–39.

Scholliers, P. (1996). Workers' Time for Cooking and Eating in Nineteenth- and Twentieth-Century Western Europe. *Food and Foodways,* 6(3–4), 243–60.

Serulnikov, S. (2017). Pobreza y revuelta de subsistencia: los saqueos de 1989 en Argentina. *Historia Social*, 88, 63–85.

Sharan, A. (2020). *Dust and Smoke: Air Pollution and Colonial Urbanism, India, c.1860–c.1940*. New Delhi: Orient BlackSwan.

Shōbei, S. (1966). The Rice Riots and the Social Problems. *Developing Economies*, 4(4), 516–34.

Silva, J. L. M. Da (2014). Alimentação e transformações urbanas em São Paulo no século XIX. *Almanack: Guarulhos*, 7, 81–94.

Smith, B. J. (2020). Food and the Mississippi Civil Rights Movement: Re-reading the 1962–1963 Greenwood Food Blockade, *Food, Culture & Society*, 23(3), 382–398.

Snitkofsky, V. (2013). Impactos urbanos de la Gran depresión: el caso de la Villa Desocupación en la ciudad de Buenos Aires (1932–1935). *Cuaderno urbano: Espacio, Cultura, Sociedad*, 15(15), 93–109.

Solt, G. (2014). *The Untold History of Ramen: How Political Crisis in Japan Spawned a Global Food Craze*. Berkeley: University of California Press.

Soluri, J. (2003). Banana Cultures: Linking the Production and Consumption of Export Bananas, 1800–1980. In S. Striffler and M. Moberg, eds., *Banana Wars: Power, Production, and History in the Americas*. Durham: Duke University Press, pp. 48–79.

Steege, P. (2007). *Black Market, Cold War: Everyday Life in Berlin, 1946–1949*. Cambridge: Cambridge University Press.

Striffler, S. (2007). *Chicken: The Dangerous Transformation of America's Favorite Food*. New Haven: Yale University Press.

Striffler, S. & Moberg, M., eds. (2003). *Banana Wars: Power, Production, and History in the Americas*. Durham: Duke University Press.

Sullivan, J. W. (1913). *Markets for the People: The Consumers Part I*. New York: Macmillian.

Talbot, J. M. (1997). The Struggle for Control of a Commodity Chain: Instant Coffee from Latin America. *Latin America Research Review*, 32(2), 117–35.

Tamārī, S. & Turjman, I. S. (2011). *Year of the Locust: A Soldier's Diary and the Erasure of Palestine's Ottoman Past*. Berkeley: University of California Press.

Tanielian, M. (2012). The War of Famine: Everyday Life in Wartime Beirut and Mount Lebanon (1914–1918), PhD dissertation, University of California at Berkeley.

Thelen, T. (2006). Lunch in an East German Enterprise – Differences in Eating Habits as Symbols of Collective Identities. *Zeitschrift für Ethnologie*, 131(1), 51–70.

Tinsman, H. (2014). *Buying Into the Regime. Grapes and Consumption in Cold War Chile and the United States*, Durham: Duke University Press.

Tocancipá-Falla, J. (2006). Cafés en la ciudad blanca: identidad, crisis cafetera y el restablecimiento del orden social en Colombia. *Revista de Estudios Sociales*, 1(25), 67–79.

Tormo-Santamaría, M. & Bernabeu-Mestre, J. (2020). Making a Virtue of Necessity: Food Education and Gastronomy in the Spanish Civil War and Post War Period (1936–1952). *International Journal of Gastronomy and Food Science*, 21, 1–7.

Tsipursky, G. (2016). *Socialist Fun: Youth, Consumption, and State-Sponsored Popular Culture in the Soviet Union, 1945–1970*. Pittsburg: University of Pittsburg Press.

Turner, K. L. (2014). *How the Other Half Ate: A History of Working-Class Meals at the Turn of the Century*. Berkeley: University of California Press.

Vasconcelos, F. A. G. (1999). Os Arquivos Brasileiros de Nutrição: uma revisão sobre produção científica em nutrição no Brasil (1944 a 1968). *Cadernos de Saúde Pública*, 15(2), 303–16.

Vega Jiménez, P. (2002). Cafeterias josefinas (1890–1930): cultura urbana y sociabilidad. *Revista de Historia de América*, 131, 81–115.

Villafuerte, G. P. (2012). Aspectos generales de la inmigración y la demografía china en el Perú (1849–1903). *Historia 2.0: Conocimiento Histórico en Clave Digital*, 2(4), 126–40.

Wang, G. (2022). A Myth of Modernity: The Market Hall Reforms in China, 1900s–1940s. *Urban History*, 50(4), 773–798.

Weber, H. (2013). Towards "Total" Recycling: Women, Waste and Food Waste Recovery in Germany, 1914–1939. *Contemporary European History*, 22(3), 371–97.

Weinreb, A. (2017). *Modern Hungers: Food and Power in Twentieth-Century Germany*. Oxford: Oxford University Press.

Yan, Y. (2000). Of Hamburger and Social Space: Consuming McDonald's in Beijing. In D. Davis, ed., *Consumer Revolution in Urban China*. Berkeley: University of California Press, pp. 201–225.

Yáñez Andrade, J. C. (2016). Alimentación abundante, sana y barata: los restaurantes populares en Santiago (1936–1942). *Cuadernos de Historia*, 45, 122–30.

Yáñez Andrade, J. C. (2019). Las ferias libres y el problema de las subsistencias: Santiago de Chile, 1939–1943. *Relaciones: Estudios de Historia y Sociedad*, 40(157), 126–32.

Yao, L. (2017). Nationalism on Their Own Terms: The National Products Movement and the Coca Cola Protest in Shanghai, 1945–1949. *Modern Asian Studies*, 51(5), 1439–468.

Yuan, Y. (2018). La comida china en el Perú: una nueva identidad multiétnica. *Religación: Revista De Ciencias Sociales y Humanidades*, 3(10), 128–38.

Yūko, F. (2022). Urban Riots and the Everyday Practice of Male Laborers in Prewar Japan. *Journal of Urban History*, 48(5), 1031–45.

Zavisca, J. (2003). Contesting Capitalism at the Post-Soviet Dacha: The Meaning of Food Cultivation for Urban Russians. *Slavic Review*, 62(4), 786–810.

Zazueta, M. del P. (2011). Milk against Poverty: Nutrition and the Politics of Consumption in Twentieth-Century Mexico, PhD dissertation, Columbia University.

Zenteno Roldán, C. (2014). Una comparación de género en el trabajo de figones, fondas y restaurantes: ciudades de México y Puebla, 1910–1920, MA thesis, Benemérita Universidad Autónoma de Puebla.

Zinkhan, G. M., Fontenelle, S. de M., and Balazs, A. (1999). The Structure of São Paulo Street Markets: Evolving Patterns of Retail. *The Journal of Consumer Affairs*, 33(1), 3–26.

Zweiniger-Bargielowska, I. (2017). Food Consumption in Britain during the Second World War. In H. Berghoff, J. Logemann, and F. Römer (eds.), *The Consumer on the Home Front: Second World War Civilian Consumption in Comparative Perspective*. Oxford: Oxford University Press, pp. 76–94.

Acknowledgments

This work is genuinely a transnational collaborative effort. We thank the California State University, Fresno and El Colegio de México for their institutional support. We benefited immensely from the following awards, "Center for Latin American Studies Stanford Library Access Grant for Minority Serving Institutions" and "Fondo de Apoyo Colmex de Investigación (FACI), 2021–2023." Many thanks to our colleagues for their help, insights, and challenging questions, including Luis Aboites Aguilar, Lori Clune, Reynaldo De los Reyes, Aurora Gómez-Galvarriato, Netzahualcóyotl Gutiérrez, Danny Kim, Andrea Lluch, Maritere López, Carlos Marichal, Paolo Riguzzi, Ariel Rodríguez, Julia Shatz, and Odalis Valladares Chamorro. Annabella España-Nájera read parts of the manuscript, we are thankful for her generosity and detailed comments. We are grateful to Camilo Mason for his invaluable help from Buenos Aires. Maribel Vasconcelos from Berlin and Carla Xochitl León Cortés from Mexico City assisted us with this project. We thank the anonymous reviewers for their detailed comments and suggestions on the manuscript, and Michael Goebel for shepherding this book through the publishing process. This Element draws largely from the Latin American historiography on standard of living, class struggle, and urban multitudes. We dedicate this work to the academics who introduced these concepts to us; we hope to have made justice to their scholarship.

Cambridge Elements ≡

Global Urban History

Michael Goebel

Graduate Institute Geneva

Michael Goebel is the Pierre du Bois Chair Europe and the World and Associate Professor of International History at the Graduate Institute Geneva. His research focuses on the histories of nationalism, of cities, and of migration. He is the author of *Anti-Imperial Metropolis: Interwar Paris and the Seeds of Third World Nationalism* (2015).

Tracy Neumann

Wayne State University

Tracy Neumann is an Associate Professor of History at Wayne State University. Her research focuses on global and transnational approaches to cities and the built environment. She is the author of *Remaking the Rust Belt: The Postindustrial Transformation of North America* (2016) and of essays on urban history and public policy.

Joseph Ben Prestel

Freie Universität Berlin

Joseph Ben Prestel is an Assistant Professor (wissenschaftlicher Mitarbeiter) of history at Freie Universität Berlin. His research focuses on the histories of Europe and the Middle East in the nineteenth and twentieth centuries as well as on global and urban history. He is the author of *Emotional Cities: Debates on Urban Change in Berlin and Cairo, 1860–1910* (2017).

About the Series

This series proposes a new understanding of urban history by reinterpreting the history of the world's cities. While urban history has tended to produce single-city case studies, global history has mostly been concerned with the interconnectedness of the world. Combining these two approaches produces a new framework to think about the urban past. The individual titles in the series emphasize global, comparative, and transnational approaches. They deliver empirical research about specific cities, while also exploring questions that expand the narrative outside the immediate locale to give insights into global trends and conceptual debates. Authored by established and emerging scholars whose work represents the most exciting new directions in urban history, this series makes pioneering research accessible to specialists and non-specialists alike.

Cambridge Elements ☰

Global Urban History

Elements in the Series

A full series listing is available at: www.cambridge.org/EGUB

Printed in the United States
by Baker & Taylor Publisher Services